Praise for *The Essential HR Handbook:*

"Since publication of the first edition, *The Essential HR Handbook* has been read and discussed by more than seventy-five new managers, who participate in our Managers' Round Table program. The information, ideas, and resources in this 10th anniversary edition will continue to enhance this program and provide ongoing value for our managers."
—Allyn Gutauskas, human resource manager,
Farmington Country Club

"Since its publication in 2008, I have bookmarked or stuck post-it notes on the pages of *The Essential HR Handbook* I refer to most often. At this point, I might just as well have tagged every page! In my role as the singular HR person for multiple organizations over the last twenty years, I have found that a reliable and easy to use HR resource is an extremely valuable tool. *The Essential HR Handbook* covers the gamut of topics and issues that HR professionals face. The book covers HR issues from start to finish in a logical and easy to use format. This book is a 'must have' for all HR professionals, especially those who run a department of one."
—Helen Elmore, SHRM-SCP, director of
finance and administration

"An invaluable resource! This edition of *The Essential HR Handbook*, with the most current information about recruitment and selection, technology, performance management, and much more, is a must-have, handy reference for anyone who deals with human resource issues."
—Cornelia Gamlem, author, *The Big Book of HR,
The Essential Workplace Conflict Handbook, The Conflict
Resolution Phrase Book,* and *The Manager's Answer Book*

"Sharon and Barbara have done it again! This new edition of *The Essential HR Handbook* has been completely updated to reflect the latest trends and realities in the workplace—from telework to employee wellness programs to how to use social media as part of your recruitment process. As with the first edition, this manual is filled with useful information and resources. It should be in your bookcase. I guarantee you will find it useful."
ncy Kelly, MHS, executive director,
Health Volunteers Overseas

"Now more than ever, leaders need both a strategic and practical guide to help them effectively manage human resources. *The Essential HR Handbook* meets this need through the authors' smart and focused presentation of current HR information, challenges and solutions. This book belongs in a new manager's toolkit!"

—Mary Camuto, MC Consulting, author,
Make the Most of Your Workday

"*The Essential HR Handbook* is a vital resource for today's leaders, providing meaningful guidance on human resources issues, along with useful scenarios and practical tools. The book has been a valuable reference tool for many years, and the authors' philosophy of lifelong learning is reflected in their highly substantive and timeless content."

—Susanne Knight, office administrator,
Los Angeles, Skadden, Arps, Slate, Meagher & Flom LLP

"I strongly encourage anyone with HR responsibilities to explore this resource."

—Anne Tomkinson, director of certification
for Washington, DC SHRM

"*The Essential HR Handbook* should be a required book in every office. From those thrust into HR duties, to the manager who needs an occasional reference volume, this multipurpose handbook will guide the way. This second edition is a testament to the continued need for such a comprehensive resource to navigating the HR field."

—Christina Lambert, SHRM-CP, manager of human resources and
administration, American Land Title Association

"In the knowledge economy, there is no more important resource than talent so understanding how best to manage talent should be the highest priority of any successful business. I highly recommend Sharon Armstrong and Barbara Mitchell's updated *The Essential HR Handbook* to not only HR professionals, but also to today's C-level executives as they seek to understand how to recruit, retain and upskill their workforce. Armstrong and Mitchell's concise and well-researched material is easily digested and applied. I have valued their earlier edition, and have found their updates to the *Handbook* to be extremely pertinent and enormously helpful. Do yourself a favor and keep this book close as I do. You will find yourself reaching for it often."

— Erinn Gray, vice president Global Human Resources, Trintech

TENTH ANNIVERSARY EDITION

THE ESSENTIAL
HR HANDBOOK

A QUICK AND HANDY RESOURCE FOR ANY MANAGER OR HR PROFESSIONAL

- ✓ Create Positive Relationships Between Employees and Managers

- ✓ Benefit from Multigenerational and Diverse Workplaces

- ✓ Develop Attractive and Fair Compensation Packages

- ✓ Manage Hirings and Firings With Minimal Legal Risk

- ✓ Integrate Workplace Flexibility and Telework

SHARON ARMSTRONG and BARBARA MITCHELL

CAREER
PRESS

This edition first published in 2019 by Career Press, an imprint of
Red Wheel/Weiser, LLC
With offices at:
65 Parker Street, Suite 7
Newburyport, MA 01950
www.redwheelweiser.com
www.careerpress.com

ISBN: 978-1-63265-139-6
Library of Congress Cataloging-in-Publication Data
available upon request.

Cover design by Jeff Piasky
Interior by Lauren Manoy
Typeset in Minion Pro and Helvetica Neue

Printed in Canada
MAR
10 9 8 7 6 5 4 3

DEDICATION

This book is dedicated to my father, Charles B. Scott, who taught me the true meaning of perseverance.
—Sharon Scott Armstrong

This book is dedicated to my parents, Anne and Tom Mitchell. I wish they were here to celebrate this achievement with me.
—Barbara Mitchell

ACKNOWLEDGMENTS

Most people understand that writing a book takes a village! There are many folks behind the scenes who helped us, so there are some thank-yous due.

Susan Devereaux skillfully and kindly edited our thoughts and words while remaining calm and put the final manuscript together in her highly professional way; Paul Mickey who contributed the updated legal chapter; Mike Strand who contributed two chapters, aided by Chris Serrano, whose help in researching the benefits chapter is greatly appreciated.

Others who deserve thanks for their contributions and support are Richard Armstrong, Cornelia Gamlem, and Joyce Oliner.

Thanks to our wonderful literary agent, Marilyn Allen, and the team at Red Wheel/Weiser for their support and confidence in us.

To paraphrase the words of William Butler Yeats, "Think where man's glory most begins and ends, and say our glory was we had such friends."

Sharon Armstrong
Barbara Mitchell
Washington, DC

CONTENTS

INTRODUCTION

*I am convinced that nothing we do is more important
than hiring and developing people. At the end of
the day you bet on people, not on strategies.*

—*Lawrence Bossidy*

Welcome to the updated version of *The Essential HR Handbook*. So much has changed since the original was published, but one thing remains the same: It is still a challenge to hire, engage, develop, and retain the best talent available! This book is designed as a resource for anyone who manages people, and that includes managers and business owners as well as human resources professionals. ·

Use this book as a reference document. Each chapter stands alone so you can pick it up and read it when you need it. When it makes sense, we've indicated where another chapter links to the one you're reading.

Some organizations have renamed their Human Resources units "People" or "Human Capital" departments to emphasize the importance of their paramount resource. They know that without good people management, nothing else matters.

Today, more than ever, leaders of successful organizations understand the importance of good human resources principles and practices for maintaining a healthy business. They expect their managers to integrate good human resources management into their day-to-day work.

In fact, in order to survive in today's increasingly challenging world of work, managers have to be lifelong learners. They have to be open, not only learning new things, but also incorporating those things in their everyday approach to work. These two behaviors are among the most critical for honing managerial skills.

That sounds simple, but we know human resources is a complex field. HR tools and techniques draw on a wide and growing body of knowledge and requirements. The challenge for managers is to stay informed of the field's best practices.

What does "human resources" mean today? It is the process of acquiring, training, appraising, and compensating employees while attending to their concerns about labor relations, health and safety, and fairness.[1]

This book provides practical information, tools, and techniques to help managers and HR professionals excel.

When Joe Gibbs, former coach of the NFL's Washington Redskins and multiple NASCAR champion, was asked to describe the differences between professional football and professional car racing, he replied, "There is none; it's all about the people."[2]

Now that's a worthy mantra for managers and HR professionals: It's all about the people.

Disclaimer

The Essential HR Handbook is published only as an informational guide. The reader should keep in mind that although it is designed to provide accurate and current information on employment law compliance issues as of the date of publication, the information contained herein is general in nature and is not intended to be relied upon as legal advice. Laws and regulations are not static, and they frequently change. Neither the information in this book, nor any information found on the Internet, should be a substitute for legal advice. The resolution of each circumstance should ultimately be determined on a case-by-case basis, depending on the particular facts, and legal counsel should be sought as appropriate.

1

STRATEGIC HR

*Strategy connects the purpose and values of your organization
with those of its customers and other external shareholders.*
—*Tony Manning,* Making Sense of Strategy

If you don't know where you're going, how will you know when
you get there? That's why every organization needs a strategy for
planning its future, and HR is a big part of that planning process.

Organizational strategy

Managers are responsible for allocating resources to achieve their
organization's stated goals, and this is where organizational strategy comes into play. Successful management of resources depends

on effective planning. Managers need to set the organization's strategic direction and develop a plan to implement the strategy.

That plan defines the organization's path into the future, and implementing it involves making decisions about the allocation of resources to reach the goals.

Organizational resources include intellectual capital, products, and financial capital, but the most important resource is human capital—the people who make it all happen. And because most organizations spend the largest percentage of their dollars on their labor force, firms that align their people strategies with their organizational strategies are the most successful.

The strategic planning process begins by determining what the organization wants to achieve throughout a reasonable period of time. In the past, standard business practice was to plan for long periods, such as five, ten, or twenty years—but in today's volatile business climate, most organizations plan for shorter periods such as one, three, or at most, five years.

For your organization to remain competitive, it is essential to revisit your strategic plan frequently, and explore the business climate in your organization's field to understand changes that may affect your organization and its strategy. Strategy development involves evaluating the organization's current business situation and determining where it wants to go in the future. Managing strategy is never "cast in concrete"—it is a continuous, recurring process.

Developing a strategic plan

The most enlightened organizations include human resources (HR) in the development of the strategic plan, so that the human resources plan can link directly to the strategic plan (discussed later in this chapter).

The typical approach to strategic planning is a three-step process:
1. Establish why the organization exists, its mission.

2. Define what you want the organization's near future to be.

3. Establish what needs to be done—and what needs to be done differently—to reach the stated objectives.

Crafting a mission statement

Organizational strategy consists of concisely, clearly, and carefully communicating to everyone in the organization where the organization is headed, which is the first step in creating a mission statement. This document describes what the organization is today, and what it values, in succinct and measurable terms. Mission statements are shared with employees, clients, and customers.

Elements of a Mission Statement

Mission statements should be succinct and easy for employees, customers, and the general public to understand. Some of the elements to consider as you craft a mission statement include your organization's:

✓ Desired image in the marketplace.

✓ Target market for products or services.

✓ Products or services (described).

✓ Local, national, or global reach—where your clients are located.

When you're developing a strategic plan, start by asking a series of questions that will produce the information you need to take the next step in defining the organization's future direction. Here are some sample questions:

✓ What are your plans for growth?

✓ What is your ethics statement?

✓ What challenges are you facing today?

✓ What are your competitors doing that you aren't doing?

✓ What sets you apart from the competition?

- ✓ What changes have occurred in your industry or service area?
- ✓ How has globalization affected your organization?
- ✓ Have your competitors entered the global market?
- ✓ Are there opportunities outside your current market to consider?
- ✓ Is your technology up to date?
- ✓ What effect has technology had on your customers, members, or employees?
- ✓ Have your customers' or members' expectations changed?
- ✓ What are you doing to retain any competitive advantage you have?
- ✓ What are your distinctive competitive strengths, and how does the plan build on them?
- ✓ How will changes in your strategy affect your employees?
- ✓ Do you have the people resources you need to reach your desired goals?
- ✓ What effect will the changing demographics have on your strategy?
- ✓ What legal or regulatory changes do you anticipate that may affect your strategy?
- ✓ How and why is this plan different from the previous one? Were all your previous elements completed? If not, why? What could you have done to complete that element?
- ✓ How different is your strategy from those of your competitors, and why? Is that good or bad? What do you know about your competitors' strategies?
- ✓ How accurate have your past budgets and projections been? What could have made them more accurate and how will you modify your budgeting process, if needed?
- ✓ Who will measure the outcomes of the strategy, and with what tools? How often will you monitor progress?

After answering these questions, you can determine how the organization will capitalize on its strengths, eliminate or minimize its weaknesses, exploit opportunities, and defend against threats. This is called a SWOT analysis (strengths, weaknesses, opportunities, and threats) and should be something you do annually.

Putting your strategic plan in motion

If the organization sets out a good strategic direction and sets goals and measurements to ensure the goals are met, it can envision its future.

But after the vision is set forth, nothing will happen without an implementation strategy. This is where responsibilities are determined and accountabilities defined. A timeline should be created, and milestone reviews should be scheduled, so that the strategic plan is constantly in front of the leadership and discussed at staff meetings. The timeline should be reviewed and updated in order to keep it as current as possible.

Communicating the plan

Once the strategic plan is developed and easily understood, it is extremely important to share it with the employees. This can be in writing, sent as an email from the leader of the organization, or communicated in person at an "all staff" meeting. How the message gets out isn't nearly as important as the fact that it is communicated. Employees need to know where their organization is headed, and how the work they do fits into the plan; this is especially important for your Millennial employees. They will leave if it's not readily apparent to them how their work impacts your mission.

Linking HR planning to the strategic plan

Organizations that link the overall strategic plan to their plans for finding and keeping employees tend to be the most successful in today's competitive marketplace. After an organization's strategic plan is in place, it is important to identify the roles the human resources department will play in achieving the organization's goals.

Once the strategic areas that will affect employees are identified, the planners need to determine whether the organization lacks any resources that will cause problems in the implementation phase.

It is at this point in the process that HR issues—a critical element in the strategic plan—really come into play. Organizations that involve HR in the strategic planning process soon learn that issues about people have an effect on nearly every organizational activity.

For example, if the plan calls for building a new manufacturing facility in South America, it is probably HR that will need to research labor markets and union activity in different countries, look at compensation plans, investigate the process for obtaining work permits and visas for US nationals, research applicable benefit plans, and gather data on whether the organization's current health plan covers workers outside of the country.

If growth is projected in the strategic plan, HR should consider creating a workforce plan. This involves looking at the current workforce in depth and asking questions such as:

✓ What are the strengths and areas of concern with the current workforce?

✓ Who is eligible to retire?

✓ Are there current employees with performance issues?

✓ Does the projected growth mean additional workers will be needed?

✓ What skills and abilities—technical, administrative, managerial, and leadership—are needed to accomplish the work?

✓ Are there gaps in the current skills of the workforce? What will be required to achieve the new strategic direction?

Once these questions are answered, HR can address how gaps can be filled. For example, if the strategy involves increasing the number of technical employees in a particular department, some solutions might be:

✓ Hiring new employees.

✓ Training existing employees.

✓ Transferring employees from another location.

✓ Doing all of the above.

If the choice is to hire new employees, the organization needs to plan how to onboard them into the workplace culture to make their transition into the organization as smooth as possible so that they can be productive.

Key Recommendations for Succession Management[1]

Understand what is unique about your organization.

Recognize that subject matter experts have special challenges when it comes to succession management—it's not as easy to see where they might fit into other positions.

Identify key positions and establish succession plans for key positions that identify at least one, and preferably more than one, potential successor.

Create a detailed development plan for the targeted successors.

Use leadership competency with caution; the future is imperfectly predicted.

Refine your process over time, recognizing that no succession management process is perfect.

Succession management as a workforce planning tool

Succession management is used in organizations to identify and prepare employees who have the potential skills and abilities to move into key positions when they become available. Having a succession plan generally guarantees a smooth continuation of business operations when a position becomes vacant within the organization due to a promotion, resignation, transfer, or death.

Succession management is a comprehensive process that begins by identifying potential successors and a development plan for each person. The goal of a succession management system is to have a pipeline of highly developed leaders across the organization who are prepared (or in the process of becoming prepared) to fill vacancies as they arise. Succession planning or management should be part of your organization's ongoing planning process and must be linked to your performance management system (see Chapter 5).

Linking HR and the organization

A typical criticism of HR professionals is that they do not understand the businesses in which they work. Critics think they are too focused on HR-related topics like compensation, benefits, and recruiting, and don't always take the time to understand marketing, finance, and business operations. This can cause a disconnect between the HR staff and other organizational leaders.

Although HR is increasingly complex, it is not a stand-alone function. For HR professionals to be true business partners, they must learn as much as possible about the operation of their organization's business. Studying business plans, strategic plans, annual reports, and other written documents is one of the best ways to do this; so is networking with others in the organization.

If you're new to an organization or new to your job, a great way to learn more about your firm and get to know others is to make a list of people with whom you need to work or interact and schedule a meeting with each one. You may want to do these meetings over coffee or lunch so that you're both more relaxed than you might be in a conference room. Before your meeting, put together a series of questions to get the conversation started. Most people enjoy sharing their expertise, and if you approach these conversations properly and respect colleagues' busy schedules, this strategy can be very effective. Possible questions include:

✓ How long have you been with the XYZ organization?

✓ What about this organization attracted you to it?

✓ What has been your greatest challenge at XYZ?

✓ What has been your greatest success?

✓ What keeps you up at night?

✓ How does your department fit into the organization's overall mission?

✓ How can the HR function help you and your staff achieve your goals?

✓ What has XYZ's HR function done well in the past, and where can it improve?

✓ Can you recommend books or other reference material so that I can learn more about what you do as [position]?

✓ Is there anything else you can tell me that will help me be the best possible business partner for you and your department?

These conversations should be dialogues, not interviews, and as informal as possible. Ideally, you will be asked to share your background and goals as well. You can also use this interview strategy if you've been with the organization for a while and get promoted. Your new level of responsibility will require you to function differently, and getting to know your peers will be helpful down the road as you work together for the good of the organization.

It is critical for people in the HR function, whether they are full-time HR professionals or managers who bear HR responsibilities, to learn the language of the organization and participate in discussions about overall strategy. This may take some time to develop, but it is extremely important in order to link the people issues to the rest of the corporate strategy.

The HR profession is complex and ever changing. HR professionals need access to information about changes in employment laws and government regulations. They also need access to others in the HR field, so they can share "best practices" or ask for help with a particular problem. The Society for Human Resource

Management (SHRM) provides a wealth of learning opportunities as well as resources on its website at *www.shrm.org*. This organization also has local chapters, most of which meet monthly for professional development programs and networking.

Updated message for managers

Organizations need to set a strategic direction to know where they are headed and how they are going to get there. HR managers, along with managers of other departments, should be key players in defining the strategic plan. Once the plan is developed, attention should be paid to developing an HR plan that links to and supports the organization's strategic plan. Without the right people in the right positions, odds are the strategic goals won't be met. A succession plan also must be included in the workforce planning process to ensure the organization has successors in case of a vacancy or for growth.

Anyone who has responsibility for HR in an organization needs to understand the business the organization is in and be able to speak the language of that business. This is a key to gaining respect in the organization and adding real value to your firm!

2

TALENT ACQUISITION

*The secret of my success is that we have gone to great
lengths to hire the best people in the world.*

—*Steve Jobs*

The hiring process is critical to the success of your organization. Done well, it can build a hardworking, loyal staff and help grow your business; done poorly, it can increase turnover and stunt your staff.

Workforce planning

The most common mistake organizations make with recruiting is to hire on an *ad hoc* or, worse yet, emergency basis. You've signed a new client, and you need to staff up quickly. A trusted employee decides to leave, and you need to find someone immediately to do their work. Your organization is growing fast, and your current staff can't keep up with the workload. Of course, these situations can and do occur from time to time, and they're often unavoidable. But building an entire organization in this way is like cooking a gourmet meal using whatever ingredients you can find in the cupboard. Unless you get lucky every time you hire someone, you'll wind up with—quite literally—a "motley crew" who may not be able to take your organization where you want it to go.

A much better way to go about talent acquisition is to tie in your hiring with the strategic HR goals discussed in Chapter 1. The workforce plan gives you a template to follow when the time comes to fill a particular position. You'll be proactive about recruiting, not just reactive, which is bound to yield better results in both the short and long term.

Finding applicants

It used to be simple: You ran an ad in the newspaper, and applicants either mailed in a résumé or applied in person. Now, applicants also use your organization's website or one of the many online sites—from general ones such as *Indeed.com* to industry-specific ones like *Journalismjobs.com*. To stay competitive and attract applicants, you may also need to participate in job fairs, recruit at local colleges or trade schools, run ads on the radio, or hold open houses at your workplace. Depending on the level of the position you're trying to fill, you may also want to use recruiting agencies.

When you advertise or post a position, it is important to stress the benefits of working for your organization. Applicants want to know what's in it for them. Another critical element is setting your organization apart from all the others that are hiring for the same type of position: What can you tell job seekers that will excite them enough to contact your organization? Include the job requirements and what's expected of the chosen applicant to make it as easy as possible for applicants to submit their information online. Direct applicants to your website to learn more about the organization.

Don't forget about your organization's culture when it comes to posting job ads. One of the most common reasons for buyer's remorse when a new employee doesn't work out is simply because they weren't a "good fit." If you run a traditional suit-and-tie office, for example, you don't want your new employee to show up on the first day of work in crocs and t-shirt. (The opposite also applies!) It goes deeper than dress codes, however. Be honest and transparent about what kind of office you run, what kind of culture you have, and what kind of candidate you're looking for. As long as you don't violate any antidiscrimination laws (see Chapter 9), you have every right to be specific and selective about whom you hire. It's okay if you scare some prospects away with this approach; you didn't want to hire them anyway. Most applicants will appreciate your honesty, and you'll increase your chances of finding the right person in the end.[1]

Using referrals and relationships

One of the best and most cost-effective sources for applicants is an employee referral program. It produces high-quality applicants (because your current employees won't want a bad referral to reflect on them personally) and lets you gauge employee morale (because employees won't refer others if they are not happy in their jobs).

Employee referral programs can range from a simple email asking all employees to refer friends to contests with cash awards or prizes for employees whose referrals are hired.

Keeping in touch with former employees you'd like to hire again is another excellent strategy. Some of the world's largest and most successful organizations bring such "boomerangs" back by letting talented employees who leave know that they will be welcome to return. Top organizations stay in touch with these former employees by sending them announcements of new clients or awards. Then, when the time is right, they invite them back. When boomerangs return, they come with new skill sets and, typically, renewed commitment to the organization.

Recruiting online

Not surprisingly, the biggest change in talent acquisition during the past decade is how much of it is now done online. Both applicants and employers frequently use job-hunting sites like *Indeed.com* or social media sites like LinkedIn to find the ideal candidate. As we mentioned earlier, industry-specific job websites are also helpful for both employers and applicants because they weed out applicants who don't have the necessary experience or credentials. Of course, your organization's own website also has a role to play. Many organizations nowadays have a section on their website for prospective employees to express their interest in applying for a job and even to submit a résumé.

When using social media websites like LinkedIn, here are a few tips to remember:

✓ Keep expanding your own professional network, even when you're not actively trying to fill a position, so you'll always have a wide pool of candidates to draw from.

✓ Stay in contact with former employees—not only because you may want to rehire them, but also because they are a good source of referrals.

✓ Use keywords to search for people who have the right experience, credentials, and skill sets.

✓ Create a keyword-rich profile for your organization so job hunters can search for you. Keep polishing and updating your profile to portray your organization as an industry leader and a great place to work.

✓ Join LinkedIn groups that relate to your industry, post helpful comments from time to time, and encourage your current employees to identify themselves on LinkedIn.

✓ Search for employees who have worked for your competitors in the past or other respected organizations in your industry.

✓ For a fee, you can also use LinkedIn as a paid recruiting service. LinkedIn offers a variety of recruiting services to employers, and the cost is reasonable.[2]

When it comes to using online recruiting services like Indeed or Glassdoor, dip your toe in the water by taking advantage of their free services and evaluating the results before you use paid advertisements.[3] If you can post pictures to your organization's free page, it is a great way to portray your corporate culture and workplace environment without resorting to clichés. Encourage your best employees to post positive reviews about your organization. Always respond to negative reviews by saying you're grateful to be advised of the problems raised and you're taking action to fix them. (Then really do it!) Resist the temptation to lash out against the reviewer.[4]

If your experience with Indeed and Glassdoor is positive, by all means, add them to your mix of paid listings. At the present time, Indeed is the largest network for active job seekers, while Glassdoor is the most popular for job candidate research. Using Indeed tends to bring in a larger quantity of applicants, while Glassdoor produces a higher quality—probably because Glassdoor candidates "self-select" themselves as a good fit before they apply. As a result, Indeed is usually best for finding entry-level administrative employees, and Glassdoor is usually better for filling managerial and director-level positions.[5]

Reviewing résumés

When the résumés start pouring in, be prepared with a plan for determining whom to interview. First, have a thorough understanding of the position: Identify specifically what you want the new employee to do and the results you want them to achieve. Determine which elements of performance or behavior—such as teamwork, reliability, and tolerance—are critical in this job, and what skills, abilities, and knowledge the successful applicant must have. If your list of requirements is long, prioritize them.

As you review résumés, here are some red flags to watch out for:
- ✓ No dates for previous jobs.
- ✓ Gaps in employment.
- ✓ Job-hopping with decreasing responsibilities.
- ✓ Accomplishments listed but not tied to a particular position.

When you've narrowed down the stack of résumés, you may want to do a quick screening interview by phone or video to ask very specific questions before setting up a face-to-face interview. Focus your screening interview on determining whether the applicant has the basic skills for the position and is within your salary range. To save everyone's time, let the job seeker know the range at the beginning of the call and ask whether the interview should continue. It is among the first thing applicants want to know, yet they're very reluctant to specify their most recent salary or their desired range, for fear they'll limit themselves or be dismissed as over- or underqualified.

Interviewing applicants

Once you set up an interview, find a private place to conduct it where you won't be interrupted. It is extremely important to treat applicants courteously so they feel good about the interview experience and your organization—even if they aren't selected for the position. Try to create goodwill for your organization regardless of the outcome.

Most of us have made the mistake of hiring someone who either lacked the necessary skills or didn't fit in with the organization's culture. But we can reduce the risk of doing that with behavioral interviewing—a systematic, analytical, and objective technique.

A behavioral interview is carefully planned and based on the job and its outcomes, according to the principle that past performance is the best indicator of future behavior. Specifically, it assumes that the way a job applicant has used their skills in the past will predict how they will use them in a new job. Managers should design questions to draw out candidates' stories of real-life experiences that illustrate their ability to perform the essential functions, reach the applicable goals, and excel in the job.

Good behavioral interview questions allow you to draw out the candidate's strengths, areas for development, and suitability for your open position. They also help you determine whether the applicant will fit into your work environment.

Those good questions will often start with:

✓ Tell me about a time . . .

✓ Give me an example of when . . .

✓ Walk me through . . .

✓ Describe for me . . .

For instance, if the person you hire must be *flexible*, consider asking, "Give me an example of a time when priorities were shifted. How did you react?" If *quality of work* is important, consider asking, "Can you tell me about a time when your boss was not satisfied with an assignment you completed?"

Make sure that interview questions do not solicit information that employers are legally barred from considering in the hiring process, such as age, gender, religion, race, color, national origin, and/or disability (see Chapter 9).

Sample behavioral interview questions

Here are some specific questions that will help you zero in on the qualities you want to find in the ideal candidate for the job:

ABILITY TO WORK UNDER PRESSURE

✓ Describe a situation in which you were required to work under pressure and how you reacted.

✓ Describe a time when you were given a job or assignment for which you had no prior training. How did you learn to do it?

ACCOMPLISHMENTS

✓ Give an example of a time when you set a goal and met or achieved it.

✓ What are some of the obstacles you've had to overcome to get where you are today? How did you handle them?

COMMUNICATION SKILLS

✓ Talk about a time when you had to communicate verbally to get an important point across, and tell me how you did it.

✓ Did you ever have an experience at work in which you had to speak up and tell other people what you thought or felt? What was the outcome?

CONFLICT MANAGEMENT

✓ What is your typical way of dealing with conflict? Give an example.

✓ Talk about a time when you had to manage a conflict or dispute among staff who reported to you or members of a team.

✓ Describe a time when you worked with others who did not work well together. How did you deal with that?

COPING SKILLS

✓ Describe a time when you were faced with problems or stresses at work and how you coped with them.

✓ Talk about a high-stress situation when you needed to keep a positive attitude. What happened?

DEALING WITH DIFFICULT PEOPLE

✓ Talk about a time in the past year when you had to deal with a difficult team member. How did you handle the situation and what did you learn from it?

✓ Describe the worst customer or coworker you have encountered and how you dealt with him or her.

DECISION-MAKING

✓ Have you ever had to refrain from speaking or making a decision because you did not have enough information? What happened? What did you learn from this experience?

✓ Describe a decision you made within the past year that you're proud of.

DELEGATING

✓ Give an example of an instance in which you delegated a project effectively.

✓ Talk about a time when you were given a vague assignment yet completed it successfully. What was the situation? What, specifically, did you do?

INITIATIVE

✓ Give an example of a time when you had to go above and beyond the call of duty to get a job done.

✓ Have you ever worked on a difficult assignment with few or no resources? What did you do? What was the result?

LEADERSHIP

✓ Have you ever had difficulty getting others to accept your ideas? What was your approach? Did it work?

✓ Describe a situation in which you had to change your leadership style to have the impact you desired.

MOTIVATION

✓ How do you motivate people? Give a specific example of something you did that helped build others' enthusiasm.

✓ How have you motivated yourself to complete an assignment or task you did not want to do?

PERSISTENCE

✓ When has your persistence had the biggest payoff?

✓ Give an example of an important goal and describe your progress in reaching it.

PERSUASION

✓ Summarize a situation in which you persuaded others to take action or to see your point of view.

✓ Describe a time when you used facts and reason to persuade someone to take action.

PROBLEM-SOLVING

✓ Give an example of how you used your fact-finding skills to get information you needed to solve a problem. How did you analyze the information and reach a decision?

✓ Did you ever have to seek out "experts" in your organization to understand something? How did you do it? What were the results?

Process improvement

✓ Describe a couple of specific examples of when you made something better or improved a service or product. How did you do it?

✓ Have you ever recognized a problem before your bosses or coworkers did? What did you do?

Supervision

✓ How many people have you supervised? If we talked to them, what three things would they say about your managerial style?

✓ Describe a situation in which a staff member was not performing up to expectations. How did you handle it?

Teamwork

✓ How do you turn people who work for you into a team? What has worked? What hasn't? Give specific examples.

✓ Describe a time when you worked with someone who did things very differently from how you did them. How did you get the job done?

Questions alone—even great ones—do not make an interview successful! So what does? The interviewer's capacity for listening effectively, avoiding quick judgments, accepting silences, and remaining objective.

You've already established your standards for evaluating the candidates; the following form can help make sure your evaluation is objective and systematic.

Suggested format for interviews

Conducting interviews will be easier and more effective if you follow the same format and agenda every time, rather than trying to "wing it" with each new applicant. Here's a suggested format for your interviews:

Applicant Evaluation Form

Applicant's name:
Interviewer:
Position:
Date:

TECHNICAL SKILL	EXCELLENT			POOR	
[Criterion]	5	4	3	2	1
[Criterion]	5	4	3	2	1
[Criterion]	5	4	3	2	1
Comments:					

EDUCATION	EXCELLENT			POOR	
[Criterion]	5	4	3	2	1
[Criterion]	5	4	3	2	1
[Criterion]	5	4	3	2	1
Comments:					

WORK HABITS	EXCELLENT			POOR	
[Criterion]	5	4	3	2	1
[Criterion]	5	4	3	2	1
[Criterion]	5	4	3	2	1
Comments:					

✓ Set the tone. Make the candidate feel comfortable and establish rapport.

✓ Let the candidate know you will ask questions about their workplace behavior and take notes, and there will be time to ask questions after you've completed yours.

✓ Ask your prepared behavioral interview questions. Politely return to the original question if the candidate's answer is evasive. If the response is incomplete, ask follow-up questions.

✓ Describe the position and the organization. (Don't describe the position in detail before this point because seasoned interviewees will just parrot your words to prove they are the ideal candidates.)

✓ Respond to the candidate's questions.

✓ Explain the next step in the process and the timeline for the employer's decision. Never give an applicant reason to believe he or she is either a shoo-in or already rejected.

✓ Close the interview by asking, "Is there anything else you think we should know that we haven't already discussed?"

✓ Thank the applicant for his or her time—and remember, every applicant is a potential customer.

Some organizations rely on pre-employment testing to evaluate applicants' skills and abilities. Before you conduct any test, check with your firm's labor attorney to ensure that every question is work-related and nondiscriminatory.

Video interviews

More and more organizations nowadays are making use of video interviews—both as an initial screening tool and to help make the final hiring decision. The largest company in the video interviewing business, HireVue, did more than two million video interviews in 2016, up from just 13,000 five years earlier. Nine out of ten video interviews were "on demand," meaning there was no live interviewer on the other end. The videos were stored electronically for later review by HR and the hiring managers.[6]

Video interviews have both pros and cons for the employer. On the plus side, they are inexpensive, efficient, convenient, and flexible. They are standardized, so managers can watch a number of different candidates answer the same set of questions. You and your hiring managers can go back and review the videos as often as you want. And they give you some insight into how the candidate performs under pressure in unusual circumstances.

On the negative side, they are prone to technical glitches. You don't have the advantage of face-to-face interaction, which can help reveal a person's character through body language, handshake, and eye contact. Candidates who are not actively looking for a job may hesitate to record a video interview for fear that the video could fall into the wrong hands.[7] Perhaps most importantly, many applicants don't think video interviews give them a fair shake. One candidate told the *Chicago Tribune,* "It was honestly pretty horrible. More like a game show than an interview."[8]

Nevertheless, video interviews aren't going away anytime soon. In our opinion, they should be used as an initial screening tool to help weed out applicants who are clearly not right for the job. Once you've narrowed the field down to a manageable number of strong candidates, however, it's best to bring them in for a face-to-face interview.

Checking references

The last step in the hiring process, checking references, sounds easy. But it can be rife with pitfalls, roadblocks, and unpleasant surprises. By all means, don't let your enthusiasm for the candidate and your eagerness to get them on board cause you to skip this step. Think of all the high-profile cases in recent years in which people have lied about their education, military service, and previous employment in order to land a job. Better to find out about these things now than after the employee has let down or embarrassed your organization.

One of the biggest obstacles you'll face when checking references is that many previous employers are prohibited by their own HR departments from making comments that could be construed as defamatory, critical, or even complimentary. These companies take a "name, rank, and serial number" approach—only confirming that the candidate worked there, in what capacity, and for what length of time. You may have to use some ingenuity to find people willing to talk candidly and off the record. Writing in *Harvard Business Review,* Rebecca Knight suggests you should follow the advice of Priscilla Claman to seek out other sources of information, such as professional associations, past employees, and your mutual contacts on LinkedIn.[9]

Don't underestimate the importance of simply double-checking the basic facts and dates. Finding a mistake or misrepresentation at that stage is like seeing the tip of an iceberg: There are usually more serious problems below!

Updated message for managers

Attracting and retaining skilled staff is one of your most important strategic priorities.

To make a successful hire, have a clear understanding of the job, prepare targeted behavioral interview questions, and be a good listener. Your job during the interview is to objectively assess the applicant by describing the job and work environment positively and honestly, creating goodwill for your organization—whether the applicant is hired or not.

By all means, make use of new technologies such as recruiting websites, social media, and video interviews. But hiring good employees is just as much an art as it is a science. Technology can help, but there's no replacement for human contact and good judgment.

Once a candidate is hired, it's time to celebrate and onboard your new staff member!

3

ONBOARDING

You've spent a lot of time, money, and effort trying to recruit the best candidates for your job openings. You've made formal job offers, and they've accepted. Now it's time to give them everything they need to get started on the right foot, fully integrating into your organization's culture, and quickly contributing to its mission.

What is onboarding?

Onboarding is the process of helping new employees achieve the expectations and goals you had in mind when you hired them. This includes such things as feeling comfortable in their new surroundings, understanding the culture and traditions of your organization, and forming strong working relationships with their colleagues. The ultimate goal of onboarding is to turn a new "hire" into a productive "employee" as quickly and efficiently as possible. While some organizations are satisfied with a half-day orientation that consists of little more than reading the employee handbook and filling out W-2 forms, others have a formal agenda for onboarding that can last up to a year and include a variety of activities, meetings, and events. The results of such well-planned programs speak for themselves. According to the Boston Consulting Group, organizations with strong onboarding programs see 2.5 times the profit growth and 1.9 times the profit margin of those who don't.[1]

The benefits of good onboarding

Statistics show that *half* of all hourly employees leave their jobs within four months of their first day at work, and half of all salaried employees leave within eighteen months.[2] When you think of all the time and money you invested in recruiting these employees—not to mention training them—you can see why this kind of turnover would be enormously expensive for your organization.

It poses other hazards, too. In our information-based economy, where intellectual property is your most valuable asset, your organization can be irreparably damaged by an employee who walks out your door and into the arms of a competitor. Good onboarding helps prevent this from happening.

In addition to limiting turnover, there are many other benefits of a strong onboarding program: It helps new hires become productive more quickly. It establishes a stronger alignment between how your new employees do their jobs and the overall mission of your organization. It helps new hires fit in with their colleagues and become better teammates. It strengthens your corporate culture by making sure new employees understand the history, tradition, and even daily routines of your organization. It reduces the anxiety and discomfort often felt by a new employee, which can prevent them from getting up to speed quickly. And it saves the supervisor's time because there will be less "hand-holding" required.[3]

When a new employee leaves the job prematurely, it usually means one of five things went wrong:

1. There was a lack of planning.
2. The employee didn't understand the job requirements.
3. The job wasn't what the employee expected.
4. The employee didn't fit in with the organization's culture or colleagues.
5. The employee did not feel welcome from the start.[4]

A strong onboarding program can help nip all these problems in the bud and prevent a premature resignation or, worse yet, a dismissal. Many terminations that are written off as "bad hires" are actually the result of bad onboarding.

Onboarding versus orientation

Part of the reason for bad onboarding is that many employers confuse it with orientation. The two terms are often used interchangeably, but they are not the same thing. An orientation program is *part* of the onboarding process, but it's only the beginning of an ongoing series of steps that should last at least ninety days, and preferably up to a year. So let's take a look at orientation first and then at onboarding.

Orientation

The first step in facilitating a smooth transition to your workplace is an effective orientation. It's important to give new employees what they need in order to do what you've hired them to do. And they should do it in a way that complements your workplace culture.

An article in *Training and Development* magazine entitled "Successful Orientation Programs" says a successful orientation should accomplish several objectives. One of the objectives states the new employee should understand the organization, in both a broad sense (its past and present, its culture, its vision for the future) and a detailed sense (policies, procedures, and other key facts).[5]

Because that's a lot to cover, many organizations divide the material into different learning modules and present them over a period of time. Some organizations also have key staff members participate to thoroughly explain aspects of their operations—and their important connections with other areas of the firm—to new employees. However, you should avoid creating an endless "dog-and-pony show" of presentation after presentation on the new employee's first day. One of the most common criticisms of orientations is that they are boring and unproductive.

Some managers prefer to conduct their own orientations after the employee has completed one coordinated by the HR department. This reinforces what's important in the new employee's own department.

Other managers collaborate with the HR department to make sure that the orientation covers topics necessary for new hires to succeed. Here's a handy ten-step checklist of what should be included in an orientation.

Orientation Checklist

1. Write a welcome letter before the employee's first day.

2. Provide a job description and any suggested performance goals.

3. When an employee starts on the job, meet with them right away.

4. Show them the facilities.

5. Schedule computer training, if needed.

6. Assign a staff member as a "buddy."

7. Take them to lunch on the first day.

8. Meet with them at the end of the day.

9. Meet again with the employee during the first few days.

10. Have one-on-one meetings on a weekly basis for six weeks.[6]

First impressions count

Don't overlook the importance of simply making the new employee feel welcome! One of the main reasons employees leave their new jobs quickly is that they didn't feel wanted and appreciated from the start. So ask yourself what positive experience you can offer on the first day to make sure you're expressing how pleased you are to have the new employee join your team.

It all starts with simply being prepared for their arrival. Do you have a desk and computer ready? Nothing is worse than making a new employee work in the hallway or at the desk of someone who's out sick. Make sure the employee's direct-report supervisor is in the office on that day and that they're not too busy with a major project or a tight deadline. Ask other employees—especially those who will be working directly with the new hire—to drop by and introduce themselves. Better yet, walk the new employee through your facility and make those introductions yourself.

Don't forget the basics. Make sure the new employee knows your policies regarding office hours, overtime rules, vacation, sick time, holidays, and so on. Give them the proper passwords for their computer and software, and provide technology training if necessary. Give the new employee keys, identification cards, safety information, and parking passes. Take them on a tour of your facilities, show them how to requisition supplies, enter codes for using the photocopier, and so on.

What about doing actual *work* on the first day? It is a good idea to have your employee undertake some kind of meaningful task right away. But you need to strike a delicate balance. Don't give new employees "busywork" that has nothing to do with the job they were hired to do. On the other hand, don't drop them into the deep end of the pool with a major assignment to let them sink or swim. Instead, try to give an assignment that is relevant to the job, but not so difficult that it can't be accomplished during the first day or week. A sense of accomplishment is probably the best "welcome gift" you can offer to a new employee.

Orientation programming

Typically, onboarding programs consist of a one- or two-day orientation that highlights the organization's mission, policies, and procedures—and explains how to use the different information systems.

This approach can work if it gives new hires the information they need to succeed in the job. Too often, though, orientation programs focus on administrative details and lack a clear statement of how the job contributes to the company's overall success. The key is to articulate your organization's vision, mission, and values in words and actions. Make sure your organization's onboarding goals are aligned with its business objectives in the orientation.

Organizations need to shift focus from their one- or two-day orientations by HR staff to a process that involves the entire staff. Top leaders must buy into and support the effort, with HR helping to ensure that executives across the organization understand and are committed to the program, so that your overall vision and mission are adequately translated, and your hiring managers support the onboarding process.

To succeed in their jobs, new employees need to be drawn into the team and the organizational family. When new hires don't succeed, it's often because they're not a "good fit" within the culture of the workplace. Research by Recruitment Solutions shows that 47 percent of employee turnover occurs in the first ninety days.[7]

More and more employers are using technology to make the initial orientation more fun. E-learning platforms and "gamification" technology can help new employees quickly master the skills and acquire the knowledge they need to do well in their new job. For example, you can create a competition among new hires to see how many signatures they can gather from their coworkers in the first few days. Then test them to see if they can match each face with the right name. At the very least, make sure new employees don't go to lunch by themselves on the first day. If new employees are coming from out of town, ask them if there's anything you can do to assist the family with feeling at home in the new community. Specifically, a good orientation should accomplish three major goals:

1. Help new employees understand why you hired them, that is, what you saw in them that you didn't see in other candidates. This can boost morale and motivation from the start.

2. Help new employees understand your organization as a whole, what it does, and what makes it different from or better than its competitors. This kind of cultural orientation lets employees feel they're part of something bigger than themselves.

3. Help new employees understand exactly where they fit into the organization and how their efforts contribute to the success of the whole. Everyone wants to feel their job is important and makes a difference.[8]

Finally, have some kind of procedure and schedule in place for checking in with the new employee on a regular basis during the next week, month, three months, and six months. As we move from orientation to onboarding, let's pause to take a look at one of your most important orientation tools: the Employee Handbook.

The Employee Handbook

It seems like such a mundane thing, but a good Employee Handbook can rescue you from many difficult situations. A bad one can rapidly land you in legal hot water. The Employee Handbook is a great way to get your employees up to speed quickly on everything from dress codes to holiday schedules. At the very least, your Employee Handbook should cover the following points:[9]

✓ A statement explaining the doctrine of "employment at will."

✓ A statement on compliance with equal opportunity laws.

✓ A policy prohibiting discrimination and harassment.

✓ An explanation of employment classification (exempt vs. non-exempt employees) and overtime rules.

✓ Family and medical leave policies.

✓ Employee health, safety, and security issues.

✓ Attendance and leave policies.

✓ Discipline policies.

✓ Termination policies.

When it comes to discipline and termination policies, you can see why it's so important to get your Employee Handbook right. It can protect you in court, but it can also harm you. For example, if your Employee Handbook says you have a progressive disciplinary process leading step-by-step from verbal warning to termination, you *must* follow each of those steps faithfully. If you do, the court will look favorably on your case. If you skip some steps, the court could use your own Employee Handbook against you.[10] That's why we strongly recommend you hire a professional HR consultant who specializes in handbooks to write your Employee Handbook *and* get it vetted by a labor lawyer, too. Make sure your new employees sign a statement saying they read the Employee Handbook and understand it. Then keep it up to date, especially when it comes to changes in local, state, and federal labor law.

Using the "buddy system" for onboarding

One of the best ways to make sure your onboarding program continues beyond the first few days of orientation is to assign each new employee a "buddy." As the name implies, a buddy will show the new employee around the facilities, make introductions, help with training, and be on hand to answer any questions. This relationship should last at least ninety days, although it often continues on an informal basis for years. The military is particularly good at doing this, so if you have some veterans on your staff, they often make excellent onboarding buddies.

Executives should have buddies, too! Ironically, executives and upper-level managers get less help with onboarding at many organizations than lower-level employees. Perhaps the organization believes executives have so much experience that they don't need any help. Perhaps a difficult first few months is considered a "rite of passage" to weed out the weak. Or perhaps executives are expected to make a significant contribution to the organization right away.[11] But all of these expectations are not only unfair, they're also counter-productive. Hiring an executive can cost your organization hundreds of thousands of dollars. Losing an executive prematurely can cost millions. Why would you toss one of your most important employees to the lions on the first day?

That's why you should begin the onboarding process with a new executive even *before* the first day. Be honest during the interview process about the problems in your organization and how the new hire is expected to help fix them. Assign an executive "buddy" just like you would do with a non-exempt employee. Make use of outside onboarding consultants and coaches if you think they would be helpful. Perhaps most importantly, schedule some "overlap" between the new executive's arrival and the predecessor's departure—not so much that they begin to get on each other's nerves, but enough to help the new person learn the ropes.[12]

Metrics

You can't manage what you don't measure. Some key aspects to quantify are turnover, how long it takes for new hires to become productive, and employee satisfaction. Keeping track of measures such as this will provide support for developing and improving strategic onboarding programs. It's expensive to find and train new employees (some estimates say as much as half their first-year salary), so think of onboarding as a way of protecting your investment.

Updated message for managers

Developing a strategic, formal approach to onboarding will lead to greater employee retention and management. If your organization suffers from a one-size-fits-all orientation approach, and if you believe that talent is walking out your door, it makes business sense to review and strengthen your new-hire process.

It's important to acclimate new employees to the organization and its operational culture. Plan a program that will effectively welcome and engage the new employees. Make sure it's more than a rundown of administrative details; it needs to involve the entire staff and include specific measures to determine its effectiveness. And don't forget: The first impression creates a lasting impression!

4

TALENT DEVELOPMENT

*The only thing worse than training an employee and having
them leave is not to train them and have them stay.*

—*Zig Ziglar*

When it comes to talent development, the good news is that organizations are spending more on training employees than ever before—an average of more than $1,200 a year per employee when you count everything from the cost of books and manuals to the salaries of in-house training staff.[1]

Fortunately, there are more ways to train employees conveniently, inexpensively, and efficiently than ever before. New technology such as mobile devices, webinars, podcasts, videos, online courses, social media, and "gamification" make learning easy, convenient, and fun. Individual coaching is becoming more and more common, not just for problem employees or high-potential employees, but for everyone. And, of course, traditional classroom learning—whether it's conducted in your conference room, at a public seminar, or in the adult-education department of your local junior college—is still a time-tested and effective way to train employees. Some organizations have even created their own *in-house* corporate universities!

As Zig Ziglar's quote at the beginning of the chapter states, "The only thing worse than training an employee and having them leave is not to train them and have them stay."[2] That's why it's up to you to fight the good fight for more training, and *better* training, at your organization. Securing the enthusiastic support (not to mention the financial resources) from both upper and mid-level management will be crucial to your success. You may be surprised to learn that your employees—despite the occasional grumbling you hear from a handful of cynics—really *want* more training and *enjoy* the process. But it pays to remember that adults learn differently from children, so they should not be taught in the same way.

Adult learning theory

Since adults do indeed learn differently than children, trainers need to understand adult learning theory to help employees build skills and realize their potential growth.

Let's start with the basics. Lisa Haneberg, author of *Facilitator's Guide: 10 Steps to Be a Successful Manager: Developing Managers for Success and Excellence,* says:

> *Managers are people, adults for the most part, so it would make sense that we could apply the basic assumptions of adult learning to the art and practice of training managers, right? As a reminder, here are some of the basic beliefs about how adults learn and how trainers should use this information:*

✓ Adult learners need to feel that the new information and skills directly link to their benefits and goals. They need to be enrolled with their hearts and minds to be engaged in the learning.

✓ Adult learners respond well to real-world examples and applications. Be sure to have conversations with trainees about how principles and practices relate to their realities.

✓ Adult learners do not like being forced to attend trainings. They want to come up with the ideas for learning and development on their own or have a list of options from which to choose. Trainers should refrain from prescribing training or development. Instead, have open conversations with trainees and ask questions that allow them to discover and determine their development options.

✓ Adult learners may be defensive or feel attacked when training is recommended to them. Put your trainees in control and ask them to define their goals and the information or skills that would most help them reach those goals.

✓ Adult learners are invested in their careers and successes. They may be reluctant to share their mistakes or weaknesses. Help trainees find the right learning environments and redefine success so that open discussions and learning evoke less fear and insecurity.

✓ Adult learners own their progress and welcome clear feedback along the way. Help trainees determine how well their development is progressing and encourage them to begin applying new skills right away.

✓ Adult learners come to training or development sessions with years of previous experiences, opinions, and mindsets. Ensure that they have the opportunity to share, acknowledge, and move beyond their biases. Concepts and practices that run counter to their usual ways of being will be accepted and applied slowly. Trainers should understand and allow time for this transition to occur.

✓ Adult learners cannot be forced to learn; they must be coachable, and this is their choice. Help facilitate their progress through open and candid conversations focused on the goals they feel passionately about achieving.[3]

It helps to remember that adults learn differently from children, and different generations of adults also have different learning styles. Baby Boomers have great respect for authority and tend to thrive in a traditional classroom setting. Generation X'ers, many of whom grew up as so-called latchkey kids, respond well to training that allows them to work independently and learn on their own. Millennials are "digital natives," so they are very comfortable with training that uses new technology. Millennials have an undeserved reputation for laziness, but they respond well to training because they consider learning new skills to be a prime benefit of their employment.[4]

None of this means you have to separate employees by age group and hold different training sessions for each of them. In fact, a mixed group means that different generations will help teach each other. The Millennial can help the Baby Boomer learn how to use a new mobile app, for example, while the Baby Boomer can show the Millennial how to survive and thrive in the organization's culture. Multigenerational training is a good thing!

Needs assessment

Before any training is done, however, you should prepare a comprehensive needs assessment. First, identify what skills are needed. Next, assess your current staff against the level of those skills. There are many ways to create a training needs assessment. For example, managers can evaluate the employee's strengths and areas for development based on actual work product and personal observations.

Leah Moran Rampy, PhD, reminds us that although managers' views of employees' development needs are important, they're not comprehensive. Peers, direct reports, and customers can provide important feedback about a person's skill, behavior, and attitude. A 360-degree feedback process—involving those who work "above," "below," and "with" the employee—can enrich the assessment and show how others perceive them.

You can find a sample needs assessment, currently in use by a national trade association, on page 45.

Tailor your plan

After reviewing information about your employees' needs, develop an action plan involving instructional design (learning objectives, content, and interactive exercises) followed by implementation and evaluation. Managers can purchase off-the-shelf training programs, create the course from scratch in-house, or identify a trainer who will customize sessions according to the individuals (or departments) and their needs.

One size does not fit all. Consider whether on-the-job training, apprenticeship training, informal learning, audiovisual tools, lectures, workshops, simulated training, long-distance courses, computer-based training, public seminars, or a combination of several methods will work best.

Different learning styles also matter. Each individual learns best when trained in his or her optimal style, and the way in which information is presented influences how well a person receives, accepts, and adapts the information. Coaching and counseling should present the information in the best way for each person's learning style, and it is the manager's responsibility to construct and deliver the training accordingly.

There are dozens of different learning styles, but the following list encompasses some of those most applicable to the workplace.

✓ Some people are visual learners (they rely on visualization or creating mental images), whereas others are auditory (they rely on listening to presented information).

✓ Some prefer to talk things out rather than to analyze; others need to think and process information first, then talk about it.

✓ Some prefer to work intently on a task with no interruptions or noise; others have shorter attention spans and welcome interruptions or breaks.

✓ Some prefer to ask questions or read directions first, then plunge in, whereas others prefer to jump first, then ask questions or read directions.

✓ Some prefer "the big picture," or global perspective; others like a step-by-step, linear view.

✓ Some people solve problems quickly; others deliberate more.

Remember: Ongoing development has been recognized as an important aspect of employee retention, and it should *not* be underestimated. To quote a Chinese proverb: If you want one year of prosperity, grow grain. If you want ten years of prosperity, grow trees. If you want one hundred years of prosperity, grow people.

Coaching, mentoring, and individual development plans

One trend we've noticed in recent years is an increased emphasis on personalized training, whether that takes the form of coaching, mentoring, or Individual Personal Development Plans (IPDPs), which use a variety of different training methods for a single employee.

Coaching, in particular, has become much more common than it used to be. And it's no longer just for high-potential employees or employees who are struggling with their jobs. More and more organizations are using coaches for all employees, or encouraging employees to hire coaches on their own. Organizations are taking a page out of the playbook of professional sports by using coaches for nearly every significant position in the organization. In today's work environment, managers feel left out if they haven't been assigned a coach.

According to *The Big Book of HR* by Barbara Mitchell and Cornelia Gamlem, coaching should be part of a larger leadership development initiative and be tied to the organization's overall goals and objectives. It's very easy for an unqualified person to hang out a shingle on the Internet as a coach nowadays, so be sure to do your due diligence. When choosing a coach, look for 1) experience; 2) testimonials from satisfied clients; 3) a philosophy that fits with your organization's culture; 4) legitimate academic qualifications and/or

Sample Needs Assessment

For each of the following areas of skill, knowledge, and ability, please make two judgments. First, rate the importance of each item to your current job requirements by choosing a number from 1 to 4 (4 = very important; 3 = important; 2 = somewhat important; 1 = not important or not relevant). Second, indicate your current level of proficiency in each area, again choosing a number from 1 to 4 (4 = very proficient; 3 = proficient; 2 = somewhat proficient; 1 = not proficient).

	IMPORTANCE	PROFICIENCY
Technical skills:		
Computer literacy		
Marketing		
Writing/editing		
Strategic planning		
Finance/accounting		
Analytical/problem-solving skills:		
Decision-making		
Troubleshooting		
Research and evaluation		
Oral communication skills:		
Meeting facilitation		
Speaking/presenting		

What other issues do you need to work on to be more effective in your role?

Reproduced with permission from Ann Casso, an organizational development specialist.

certifications; and 5) an approach that resonates with your own value system. Once you've hired a coach on behalf of an employee, however, let them do the job! It is counterproductive—perhaps even somewhat unethical—to micromanage the process by looking over the coach's shoulder and asking for daily progress reports or confidential information.

A typical coaching engagement lasts between three to six months, and coaches usually meet with clients twice a month for sixty to ninety minutes. They can meet in person, on the telephone, via Skype, or any combination of these methods. The usual process consists of an initial meeting, a needs assessment, early feedback, goal development, and then a series of regular meetings that work toward the goals the client and coach have established together.[5]

Joanne Lozar Glenn, the author of *Mentor Me,* reminds us that as a manager, you have another valuable tool for training employees: mentoring. The demand for mentoring is growing, especially among younger employees. Research suggests that Millennials, in particular, have high expectations for themselves and their careers, and they learn best from the mentoring approach.[6] Your employees want mentoring in two areas:

1. The skills they need to succeed on the job. Ongoing training and development should include your one-on-one coaching, based on your own experience.

2. The skills they need to build a satisfying career. Here, you serve as both a role model and a networker for your employees. Share your own struggles and successes. Invite employees to attend important meetings with you, and then attend future meetings in your place. Expose them to other successful professionals inside and outside your organization, and encourage them to discuss their own career development.

You can also inspire employees to mentor themselves by encouraging them to be their own best advocates in the workplace. Here's how:

✓ Teach employees to recognize and play to their own strengths.

✓ Help them address their own mistakes with a sense of humor, or at least with grace.

✓ Challenge employees to increase creative control of their jobs and take a proactive approach to performance reviews.

✓ Help them build a portfolio that showcases their best work, and teach them the subtle art of self-promotion.

✓ Introduce them to a mentor other than yourself who can help them work through issues in a short-term, highly focused encounter, such as handling career plateaus or transitions, or navigating office politics.

Another tool you have at your disposal when it comes to training—one that has become more common in recent years—is the Individual Personal Development Plan (IPDP). (This is not to be confused with the Performance Improvement Plan, which is for employees who are struggling with their jobs and need to show improvement before facing discipline or termination.) The IPDP is a tool for talented employees that seeks to use the entire spectrum of training modalities in a systematic way to help employees reach their full potential. The IPDP is usually a written plan for developing specific knowledge, skills, and competencies that will be valuable for both the short-term goals of the organization and the employee's long-term career goals. The IPDP's purpose is to improve the employee's performance in current work assignments while preparing him or her for greater responsibilities in the future.[7] The plan can include every kind of training method, including mentoring, coaching, public seminars, adult-education classes, high-tech training tools, and whatever else is deemed helpful for the employee's development.

Training trends for the 21st century

Whereas leadership, supervisory skills, and customer service continue to be among the most popular employee training topics, new challenges in the workplace have increased the demand for training in areas that were less common just a few years ago. For example:

✓ Workplace violence. The sudden increase in mass shootings—especially in schools, churches, and offices—have caused many organizations to seek training on safety, security, and the prevention of workplace violence. OSHA receives more than 2 million reports of workplace violence a year, which it defines as "any act or threat of physical violence, harassment, intimidation, or other threatening disruptive behavior that occurs at the work site."[8] Many of these incidents are minor, but some are quite serious. The Bureau of Labor Statistics, for example, reported 4,679 workplace injuries in 2014, and nearly 10 percent of these were homicides.[9]

✓ Bullying in the workplace. Even if it never reaches the stage of physical violence, bullying in the workplace has also become an increasingly widespread and serious issue. According to the Workplace Bullying Institute, bullying is defined as "abusive conduct that is threatening, humiliating, or intimidating." This includes such behaviors as falsely accusing an employee of making a mistake, giving an employee the silent treatment, spreading malicious gossip about an employee, taking credit for someone else's work, or publicly humiliating an employee. The Institute says that nearly 54 million workers, or 35 percent of all employees, have been the target of workplace bullying at some point in their careers.[10] It's important to help prevent this behavior with training, because such incidents are a leading cause of employee turnover. And if they involve employees in a protected class—including racial or religious minorities, women, or older employees—they can also lead to legal action.

✓ Sexual harassment and gender/inclusion. Responsible organizations have been conducting training on sexual harassment for many years now. But recent high-profile incidents involving Hollywood producers, movie stars, and politicians have made the American public more sensitive to this issue and more apt to speak out about it—which, in turn, makes it more likely you'll need to deal with problems of sexual harassment in your organization. The same goes for issues of gender and inclusion, which could affect your organization's policies on dress codes, restroom usage, family leave, and many other matters. Effective employee training in these fast-changing areas can help prevent serious legal problems before they occur.

✓ Big data analytics. If there's one skill set that will become increasingly important in the years ahead, it will be the ability to analyze so-called "big data." We have become a society overloaded with information but sorely lacking in understanding. That's why the successful organizations of the 21st century will train all employees—not just a handful of specialists—in dealing with and understanding big data.

✓ The challenges of globalization. Another important development in training is the trend toward globalization. As more and more American organizations move jobs overseas—or do business with foreign organizations—your employees will need to be trained in such things as foreign-language skills, dealing with a remote workforce, and understanding local laws and customs. Globalization also leads to the need for more re-training and the development of new skills back home.

New technologies in training

It should be clear by now that you'll face an increasing need for employee training in the years ahead. Fortunately, there will be plenty of new technology to help you. Thanks to various e-learning technologies, employee training will become more convenient, less expensive, and more customized to individual needs than ever before.

We have seen an impact on training from teleseminars, webinars, and podcasts. In the future, look for more employee training to be done with smartphone applications, "bite-sized" training using ninety-second videos, podcasts, and even "gamification," which involves using virtual reality or augmented reality to turn employee training into something resembling a video game.

Airline pilots, for example, have been trained using cockpit simulators for years. Before long, new technology will make it possible (and affordable) to train a wide variety of employees—from truck drivers to neurosurgeons—in the same way. (For more about new technology in Human Resources, see Chapter 11.)

Evaluation

After a training session or program has been completed, senior management will have one important question for you: "Did it work?"

"It's too soon to tell," is not a satisfactory answer, even if it may be true.

That's why you need techniques for measuring and evaluating the effectiveness of employee training—not only to keep your bosses satisfied, but also to know how much more training, and what kinds of additional training, may be needed.

Assessing training effectiveness often entails using the four-level model developed by Donald Kirkpatrick.[11] According to this model, evaluation should begin with Level 1, and then, as time and budget allow, should move sequentially through Levels 2, 3, and 4. Information from each prior level serves as a base for the next level's evaluation. Thus, each successive level requires a more rigorous, time-consuming analysis, but each also represents a more precise measure of the training's effectiveness.

Level 1 evaluation: Reactions

Just as the word implies, *evaluation* at this level measures how participants in a training program react to it. It attempts to answer questions regarding the participants' perceptions, such as,

"Did they like it?" and "Was the material relevant to their work?" This type of evaluation is often called a "smile sheet." According to Kirkpatrick, every program should be evaluated at this level to provide for the improvement of a training program. In addition, the participants' reactions have important consequences for Level 2. Although a positive reaction does not guarantee learning, a negative reaction almost certainly reduces its possibility.

Level 2 evaluation: Learning

Assessing at this level moves the evaluation beyond learner satisfaction and attempts to assess the extent to which students have advanced in skills, knowledge, or attitude. Measurement at this level is more difficult and laborious than at Level 1. Methods range from formal to informal testing to team assessment and self-assessment. If possible, participants take the test or the assessment before the training and after training to determine the amount of learning that has occurred.

Level 3 evaluation: Transfer

This level measures the transfer that has occurred in learners' behavior because of the training program. Evaluating at this level attempts to answer the question, "Are the newly acquired skills, knowledge, or attitude being used in the everyday environment of the learner?" For many trainers, this level represents the most accurate assessment of a program's effectiveness. However, measuring at this level is difficult as it is often impossible to predict when the change in behavior will occur, and thus requires important decisions in terms of when to evaluate, how often to evaluate, and how to evaluate.

Level 4 evaluation: Results

Frequently thought of as the bottom line, this level measures the success of the program in terms that managers and executives can understand: increased production, improved quality, decreased costs, reduced frequency of accidents, increased sales, and even higher profits or return on investment. From a business and organizational perspective, this is the overall reason for a training program, yet results at this level are not typically addressed. Determining the results in financial terms is difficult to measure, and they are hard to link directly with training.

Updated message for managers

It's important for experienced employees to improve the skills and knowledge that help them function more effectively and grow. It is also important to bring about change in your workplace in order to continue to grow and remain competitive.

Peter Senge, author of *The Fifth Discipline: The Art and Practice of The Learning Organization,* defines these as "organizations where people continually expand their capacity to create the results they truly desire, where new and expansive patterns of thinking are nurtured, where collective aspiration is set free, and where people are continually learning to see the whole together."[12]

This is an exciting time to be involved in employee training and development. Not only has training taken on increased importance in today's organization, but there are more effective, flexible, and inexpensive ways to deliver training than ever before. Be careful, however, not to engage in training just for the sake of doing it. Remember to hold your employees accountable for the training they receive. Mere attendance is not enough. You should expect to see noticeable improvement in performance, skills, and work behavior. Meanwhile, you should accept the responsibility to take a proactive, personal approach to your employees' development. Find ways to mentor them. As in all good business relationships, mentoring is a two-way street. Be open not only to what employees need to learn, but also to what *you* need to learn from them.

5

PERFORMANCE MANAGEMENT

It's curious that we spend more time congratulating people who have succeeded than encouraging people who have not.
—*Neil DeGrasse Tyson*

A performance review, as the old joke goes, is like a fruitcake: It comes around once a year whether you want it to or not. In fact, performance reviews (or performance appraisals) have been coming around every year since 230 AD when they were first introduced in the Wei Dynasty of China as a way of rating the work of government officials.[1]

By the early 1800s, the idea of evaluating and ranking employees was so widely accepted that an owner of a cotton mill in Scotland hung a color-coded wooden block near the workstation of each employee to indicate whether their work was up to snuff or not.[2]

This cold-hearted approach to managing employees probably reached its peak in the mid-1980s when, under the leadership of CEO Jack Welch, General Electric ranked all of its employees under a numerical system and then *fired* anyone who scored in the bottom 10 percent. GE's brutal rating system, worthy of an Egyptian pharaoh, came to be known as "rank and yank." No wonder performance reviews are unpopular!

Perhaps it's no surprise that General Electric was one of the first companies to publicly question the usefulness of performance reviews and make some substantial changes in how they are done.[3] Other Fortune 500 companies such as Microsoft, Gap, Adobe, Deloitte, and Accenture followed suit. They either changed their performance review process or abolished it altogether and moved toward offering more frequent feedback to employees in place of traditional appraisal processes.[4]

Managers still need to evaluate the work of their employees. Organizations still need a system in place for determining pay raises and promotions. Performance reviews still have an important legal role to play in documenting subpar work over a period of time before an employee is disciplined or terminated. And perhaps the most compelling reason for keeping performance reviews in your organization is: Employees want them!

No, they don't *like* them. But employees have a basic human need for feedback, appreciation, and guidance. Even top executives want to know if other people think they are doing a good job. Your employees want to be told how they're doing, and you owe them that courtesy.

That's why we still believe in the fundamental value of performance appraisals. Is there room for improvement? Absolutely. Can they be streamlined, modified, and enhanced with new technology? Of course. At the end of this chapter, we'll take a brief look at both the case for radically overhauling the performance management system (or even doing away with it altogether) and the case for keeping your current system in place with some key improvements.

Meanwhile, here are four steps you can take to make your performance appraisals better—whether you choose to do formal annual "reviews" in the traditional manner or more frequent, ongoing management "check-ins," as many organizations are choosing to do nowadays.

The four components of a performance discussion

Planning and preparation

Before the meeting, make sure you're familiar with the evaluation form and the rating structure, if applicable. Whether your organization uses grades, a sliding scale, or some other kind of quantitative measure, you may need to explain how it works as well as the criteria for rating each step.

Review individual goals set during previous discussions to assess how well the employees are meeting them or met them. Do they understand your expectations? What are the employees' strengths or weaknesses? Do they contribute to the group's mission?

When you schedule the meeting, choose a day and time when neither of you is under pressure. Allow enough time for a two-way discussion, and encourage the employee to write a self-evaluation; even though it's usually optional, you should explain, in positive terms, why both evaluations are valuable. They're designed to help employees gauge their own performances and to learn how they're doing from their supervisors' point of view.

Starting the meeting

Set a warm tone—informal but professional—from the beginning so that the employee feels at ease and comfortable. However, avoid small talk, and move right into reassurance if the employee seems anxious. If you are planning to bring up any positive points, do so! That's an instant stress-reducer. But don't say it unless it's true.

Briefly outline what ground you want to cover in the meeting, in what order, how the meeting will be structured, and what you want to accomplish. Make sure the employee understands this is a two-way conversation and encourage him or her to bring up any issues you haven't mentioned.

The discussion

First, ask open-ended questions to get a general reaction. Many reviewers start with, "How do you think things have been going?" or "What would you do differently?"

Let the employee talk; listen, and try not to interrupt. You want to empower the employee, not assert your superiority.

Describe your employee's job in terms of the big picture. What is its purpose, and how does it affect, and reflect, the organization's success? Some aspects of the job are bound to be less fulfilling than others; why are they important?

Review the employee's significant accomplishments; nothing beats praise and credit for building confidence, driving discussion, and reinforcing good performance ratings.

Then you can move on to the form, if you're using one. Work your way through each section of it, using it as a tool for encouraging discussion. Remember to focus on the employee's job performance, not personal characteristics. Consider asking such questions as:

- ✓ "What have I done to help—or hinder—your job performance?"
- ✓ "What can I do in the next review period to help you achieve/improve?"
- ✓ "What conditions here enable you—or make it hard—to do your best work?"
- ✓ "What do you want most from your job?"
- ✓ "How can I help you reach your career goals?"

When you discuss areas where the employee's performance falls short, use phrases such as "I was concerned . . ." Be prepared to back up your points with specific examples, including the tangible ones you collected when you wrote the evaluation. Stay calm, and don't express your constructive criticism in such a way that you seriously disturb a good employee. Remember that, in the end, you're trying to encourage improvement.

Closing

It's just as important to end the meeting in a professional and positive manner as it was to start it that way. You want the employee to leave the discussion with a positive impression of the process.

Ask the employee to summarize the discussion you just had; make sure you are on the same page regarding the important points. If the employee introduced points you hadn't considered while writing the appraisal, apologize for your oversight and say you'd like a few days to consider how this information might affect your evaluation. If you feel a change is warranted, go ahead and make it.

Agree on a plan for the future with the employee. Write goals for the next evaluation cycle that are specific, measurable, challenging but achievable, and time-specific. You can offer to help him or her reach those goals.

Remind the employee that, if he or she has any additional reactions later, your door is always open. Close the meeting on a friendly note, and remind the employee that he or she is an important part of the team, whose performance affects your department and the organization. Encourage the employee, and be sure to express appreciation for good work and for participating in the evaluation process. If you're using a form, have the employee sign and date it.

Remind the employee that you'll continue to give feedback throughout the year and welcome any questions about his or her performance as well. Encourage the employee to come to you about any concerns or problems he or she might face in the weeks and months ahead.

The case for banishing performance reviews

As we mentioned at the beginning of this chapter, the whole idea of doing performance reviews has come under attack in recent years. More and more HR professionals and corporate executives are beginning to wonder if the review system as it is currently structured is doing more harm than good. According to the Corporate Executive Board, as many as 6 percent of all Fortune 500 companies have gotten rid of numerical rankings in their performance appraisal system.[5] Here are some of the reasons why the traditional annual performance review is falling out of favor:

✓ They are discouraging. Research at Kansas City University has uncovered a particularly disturbing fact: Even terrific employees who are open to criticism and sincerely want to get better at their jobs find reviews to be demotivating.[6] If you think you deserve a 5, for example, and your boss gives you a 4 because he believes "there's always room for improvement," you might get mad enough to start looking for another job. Millennials in particular don't like traditional performance reviews. One study showed that one out of four Millennials would rather get a new job than undergo a review.[7]

✓ Annual reviews let performance problems fester. If you notice a problem with an employee's work in February, are you going to wait eleven months until next January to mention it? It sounds ridiculous, but many passive-aggressive managers do just that. In today's fast-paced business environment where changes are taking place by the hour, it makes little sense to wait a year to make improvements in performance.

✓ They focus on the past rather than looking forward. Giving annual performance reviews is a little like trying to drive by looking in the rearview mirror. The whole idea is to improve the organization's productivity in the coming year, so why focus on what happened last year? More and more organizations are emphasizing what's known as "forward feedback" in their performance discussions.

✓ They waste time, paper, and money. Some estimates say that managers spend up to 210 hours a year preparing for performance reviews, meeting with employees, and complying with all the paperwork that the HR department requires afterward.[8] That's more than five full weeks of a manager's time! Is it worth it? One study found that they actually have a negative impact on performance about one third of the time.[9]

✓ They can be biased. Managers have a tendency to be overly fond of employees they hired themselves and highly critical of those they inherited. As a result, many employees say the review system is rigged in favor of the boss's pets. This doesn't even account for the gender, race, and sexual-orientation bias that occurs throughout society.

✓ They damage teamwork. Organizations spend a lot of time, money, and effort trying to engender teamwork among their employees. Then they go and spoil it all by using a performance-management system that ranks employees with a numerical rating, solicits gossip and finger-pointing from employees, encourages office politics and back-biting, hands out raises and promotions to some employees but not to others, and does a number of other destructive things to undermine and discourage working as a team.

Given all this (and more) it's little wonder that Professor Kevin Murphy, an expert on performance appraisals, once told *The New Yorker*, "I'd like to lead a million-man march on Washington to get rid of performance reviews."[10]

But hold on a minute. Before you paint your protest sign and get on a bus for Washington, you should know there's also a case to be made for performance reviews at your organization.

The case for better performance management

The first reason for keeping performance appraisals is that you're simply not going to get rid of them. Trying to abolish performance appraisals is like trying to abolish gravity. Organizations want and need a way to evaluate employees for pay raises, promotions, guidance, improvement, discipline, and even termination. If you try to get rid of performance appraisals in your organization, you're going to create a gaping hole in your management process that demands to be filled with *something*—whether you choose to call it a "performance review" or not.

In fact, if you take a closer look at the dozens of magazine articles and research papers calling for the abolition of performance reviews, you'll find that many of them actually call for replacing performance reviews with a different *kind* of performance review. So it's really a game of semantics.

The same thing holds true for many of the organizations that have received publicity for getting rid of performance reviews. If you look closely, you'll find they haven't abolished performance reviews at all. They've streamlined them. They've added new technology. They've reduced the paperwork. They've made them less formal. They're having performance discussions more frequently than once a year. And they've made other minor tweaks and improvements in their performance management system.

So don't throw the baby out with the bathwater. Before you even think about doing away with performance appraisals in your organization, give some thought to all the good things they do. Remember: The need for recognition is a basic human desire. Failing to provide performance feedback to your employees is a major reason why employees quit or become disengaged. Employees need feedback to grow, improve, and perform at higher level. Managers need a way to communicate their expectations and goals. Performance appraisals help managers groom employees for succession planning and career advancement. Most importantly, they help every employee pull in the same direction to achieve organizational goals and objectives.

That's not to say they can't be improved, because they can. If you take all the recent criticisms of performance reviews, plus the experience of organizations that have experimented with changing them, three major areas for improvement emerge.

First, make your reviews less formal and do them more than once a year. Consider using a system of informal check-ins or discussions that occur on a quarterly, monthly, or even weekly basis. Such meetings can be much shorter and less time-consuming than an annual review. Problems can be addressed as soon as they occur, before they have a chance to fester and grow. Praise is also much more effective when the employee receives it immediately after doing a good job rather than waiting a year for a pat on the back. Try to make the meetings more casual and conversational so they'll be less intimidating to the employee and less confrontational for the manager. Ideally, both managers and employees should look forward to these discussions instead of dreading them.

Second, remove as much paperwork and red tape from the system as possible. Elements such as numerical scales and check-off boxes have outlived their usefulness. Some organizations have streamlined their system down to just a handful of simple questions to ask after the completion of every major project (what went right, what went wrong, what can be done better in the future). Try to keep the focus on future goals rather than past mistakes. Make sure those goals are short-term and achievable. New technology, including software platforms that are specifically designed for performance reviews, can help simplify and streamline your performance review process (see Chapter 11).

Third, focus on employee development. Make sure the performance review meeting is a two-way street in which the employee has ample time to address ideas and concerns. Help the employee understand that he or she must take responsibility for his or her own career advancement, but the manager is always there to help with advice and direction. When you talk to an employee about mistakes, remember that these are not occasions for discipline but opportunities for "coachable moments." We always learn more from our mistakes than from our successes, so help the employee learn how yesterday's failure will help him or her succeed tomorrow.

Updated message for managers

If something has been around for nearly 1,800 years, there are probably some good reasons for it—even if nobody likes it! That's why we believe you should *embrace* your performance management process and put your efforts into improving it rather than trying in vain to get rid of it.

The critical part of any performance management program is to make sure that ongoing conversations between managers and employees are occurring in the workplace on a regular basis. These conversations need to focus on setting measurable goals, monitoring progress, and making mid-course corrections, if needed.

Whether you decide to go with a traditional performance review system with annual meetings, numerical rankings, and reams of paperwork—or a more modern approach with frequent informal check-ins and high-tech software—is totally up to you. Your performance management system should reflect your organizational culture and goals. It goes without saying that Tesla's process may look very different from Ford's. But that doesn't mean they both can't be equally effective.

The important point is that performance discussions are a *good* thing. Managers *need* them to do their jobs well. Employees *want* them—even if they say they don't. And your organization *must* have them in order to achieve its long-term goals and objectives. So use the advice in this chapter to make your performance reviews as good as they can be.

6

BENEFITS
BY MICHAEL STRAND

Write your injuries in dust, your benefits in marble.
—*Benjamin Franklin, American statesman, scientist, philosopher,*
author, and inventor

Government-mandated benefits

Based on an evolving national commitment to provide workers with basic welfare and security, both federal and state laws
require several benefits. Individual states and other jurisdictions
may require benefits—such as minimum wage and continued
insurance after layoff or firing—that are more generous than the

federal requirements. Have your legal counsel check all relevant employment laws.

Social Security and Medicare

Social Security replaces a portion of income upon retirement, based on a formula of earnings and years worked (eligibility starts at age sixty-two). Medicare, a health insurance benefit, provides basic protection against the cost of health care (eligibility starts at age sixty-five).

Employers and employees pay equal portions of the Social Security and Medicare taxes.

> If an employee has multiple employers, it may be important to track total earnings each year because the Social Security tax is subject to a dollar limit (adjusted annually for inflation). The employer's responsibility for withholding and matching the Social Security tax ends once that limit is reached. There is no current earnings limit for the Medicare portion of the tax.

Medicaid

Medicaid is a joint federal and state program that helps with the medical costs for individuals who have limited income and resources. It also offers benefits not normally covered by Medicare such as nursing home care and personal care services. According to the Health Insurance Association of America, Medicaid is a "government insurance program for persons of all ages whose income and resources are insufficient to pay for health care."[1]

Medicaid is the largest source of free medical- and health-related services for people with low-income and disabled people. States are not required to participate in the program. Medicaid recipients must be US citizens or legal permanent residents, and may include low-income adults, their children, and people with certain disabilities. Poverty alone does not necessarily qualify someone for Medicaid.

The Patient Protection and Affordable Care Act ("Obamacare") significantly expanded both eligibility for and federal funding of Medicaid. All US citizens and legal residents with income up to 133 percent of the poverty line, including adults without dependent children, would qualify for coverage in any state that participated in the Medicaid program.

Medicare and Medicaid are the two government-sponsored medical insurance schemes in the United States and are administered by the US Centers for Medicare and Medicaid Services.

Unemployment insurance

Unemployment insurance provides compensation to qualified workers during periods of involuntary unemployment. Each state administers the premiums, claims, and payment of unemployment benefits through either a state agency or a qualified insurance company. Nevertheless, unemployment insurance laws are heavily guided by federal standards. The Federal Unemployment Tax Act (FUTA) imposes an annual tax on the first $7,000 of wages paid to each employee. The state tax depends on state guidelines, which may include the employer's unemployment-claims history.

To minimize unemployment claims, employers should: have in hand a written statement specifying the reason each employee is resigning the position (employees who are laid off will probably be eligible; eligibility for those who are fired depends on the circumstances); ensure there is sufficient cause to fire or lay off an employee; respond promptly and thoroughly to inquiries from the state unemployment agency; challenge an agency's decision to grant unemployment benefits if you believe they are not deserved; and, if necessary, present evidence at an unemployment hearing.

Workers' compensation

Workers' compensation is paid to employees injured on the job for loss of compensation and medical payments to a provider for treating the injury. States may differ on the minimum number of employees necessary to require employers' participation in the workers' compensation program. States generally administer workers' compensation through either a state agency or a qualified insurance company.

A primary purpose of workers' compensation is to relieve the employer from liability for worker injuries, so long as the employer was not negligent.

Family and medical leave

The federal Family and Medical Leave Act (FMLA) requires employers with fifty or more employees to allow eligible employees up to twelve weeks of unpaid leave during a twelve-month period for treatment of a serious health condition of the employee or the employee's immediate family, birth of a child, or the placement of a child for adoption or foster care. The employee must meet certain conditions to be eligible, as well as other requirements. (As with unemployment insurance, some states have more generous FMLA leave provisions.)

State disability income insurance

Some states require employers to provide temporary disability insurance for employees. (See more under "Disability insurance" on page 76.)

Core benefits

Nearly all employers, large and small, offer some basic benefits that provide paid time off. Somewhat less prevalent, but no less important, are health insurance, life insurance, disability insurance, and retirement plans.

Paid time off

As a societal tradition, most employers offer holidays, vacation, sick leave, and other days off to be competitive with other employers and foster a mentally healthy workforce. Organizations' paid-time-off plans are usually administered internally. Even if payroll management is not computerized, a file of basic time and attendance cards should be sufficient to adequately administer eligibility for and use of paid time off.

Holidays

Although no federal or state laws require employers to offer paid or unpaid holidays, almost all organizations do. Their selection of holidays can vary depending on the industry (construction, retail sales, trade association, civil service, and so on). The most widely observed paid holidays are New Year's Day, Memorial Day, Independence Day, Labor Day, Thanksgiving Day, and Christmas Day. Other holidays often added to the list include Martin Luther King Jr. Day, Presidents' Day, Columbus Day, Election Day, Veterans Day, the Friday after Thanksgiving, and Christmas Eve.

Whereas the observance of some holidays is designed to create three-day weekends, others occasionally fall on and are celebrated during a weekend. To address these circumstances, many employers' written policies state, "Unless otherwise notified, a holiday that falls on a Saturday will be observed on the previous Friday; a holiday that falls on a Sunday will be observed on the following Monday."

Whether to extend holiday pay to part-time employees often depends on how critical the part-timers are to the organization and the number of hours they usually work. When extending paid time off—including holidays—to part-timers, employers often prorate the time paid. For example, six hours of holiday pay for part-timers who regularly work at least thirty hours a week; four hours for those who regularly work at least twenty hours a week; and two hours for part-timers who regularly work at least ten hours a week.

Vacation

Vacation days are usually accumulated through the accrual of vacation time throughout a unit of time such as pay period, month, or year. Employers usually require advance notice and supervisor approval of accrued vacation time. They do not typically approve vacation time in excess of what has already been accrued.

Annual vacation accrual ranges between one and four or more weeks a year, depending on how long the employee has worked for the organization, the rank of position, and other factors. Although a new employee may accrue one or two weeks of vacation time in the first year, most employees have to wait three to five years or more before they accrue additional weeks.

Some organizations limit the maximum *accrual* of vacation time in order to encourage employees to take their time off, which is intended for rest and relaxation away from the workplace. The limits vary from the somewhat draconian "use or lose" policy (usually by year) to several years of accrual. Nearly all organizations treat vacation accrual as a vested benefit (the employee is paid for the accrued vacation time when he or she leaves the employer). Because of this vested financial aspect, organizational accounting must enter accrued vacation as a liability from one year to the next.

As with holidays, firms that rely heavily on their part-time employees may allow prorated vacation accrual. It is unusual, however, for organizations to prorate vacation accrual to those who work less than twenty hours a week.

Sick leave

Traditionally, sick leave is paid time off for an employee's own illness. With the advent of "family friendly" employee-benefit plans, more organizations are extending the use of sick leave to allow employees paid time off to care for other members of the immediate family when they have a temporary illness.

Typically, sick leave accrues periodically for a total of six to twelve days a year. Organizations that provide disability insurance often impose a limit on sick leave accrual—but unlike accrued vacation time, sick leave is not typically a vested benefit. Thus, there are no balance sheet ramifications to carrying over sick leave from one period to the next. And some organizations have a sick leave buy-back program, in which employees may convert a portion of accrued sick leave to vacation or cash.

Having a published policy on the use of sick leave is important to minimize the possibility of abuse. The policy should have guidelines for when and whom an employee should notify in the case of illness, and it may require supportive documentation, such as a doctor's note, if the absence is more than a specified number of days. The policy should also describe the disciplinary ramifications in the case of a persistent problem with absences for illness. And some organizations have a policy of not paying sick leave once an employee has given notice of resignation.

A major problem with sick leave is that it is often an unscheduled absence, placing a burden on other employees. Some employers are combining vacation and sick leave accrual in a paid-leave "bank." This can reduce the organization's costs for administrative time and absenteeism.

Here's an example of how an organization can convert from a vacation and sick-leave plan to a paid time-off plan. Say the former plan provided ten days of vacation and ten days of sick leave per year. Under the new paid time-off plan, half the former annual accrual of sick leave is added to the vacation leave as a vested benefit. Thus, under paid time off, each employee receives fifteen days of paid time off per year. Employees who don't use their sick leave will love this change. Employees who routinely use all or most of their sick leave will hate this change. Whom do you want to please?

It may be prudent to allow employees who have accumulated significant sick leave hours to use those hours for a limited period (say, two to three years). To still exert some control over that use, the organization may require employees who want to use the old, accumulated sick leave hours to first use two days of paid time-off hours.

Paid sick leave mandates

Gradually, more jurisdictions (county and state) are mandating paid sick leave for part-time workers. In 2018, Maryland joined eight other states and several cities and counties in adopting laws mandating that employees receive a minimum amount of paid time off for reasons related to sickness and safety.

With some exceptions, businesses in Maryland with fifteen or more employees will have to provide up to forty hours of paid sick leave to workers each year. Furthermore, those employers with fewer employees must provide the same amount of time as unpaid leave.

As an example of a paid sick leave mandate, in Maryland, employees ages eighteen and older who regularly work twelve or more hours a week are eligible for leave under the act. Employees may accrue one hour of paid sick and safe leave for every thirty worked—up to forty hours a year—and they may carry over up to forty hours of accrued leave from one year to the next. Businesses may opt to provide forty hours of leave as a lump sum at the start of the year.

The leave may be used to care for the employee's own or a family member's mental or physical illness or injury, parental leave, or issues related to domestic violence, sexual assault, or stalking.

Furthermore, under Maryland's new law, "employers with five or more employees must provide at least one hour of paid leave for every thirty hours worked, not to exceed fifty-six hours of earned paid leave in a calendar year." Employers with fewer than five employees must provide leave at the same rate—one hour for every thirty hours worked—and up to fifty-six hours of leave per year.

Maryland employers must also keep three years' worth of records on the sick and safe leave that each employee uses.

Some states and cities that currently provide paid sick leave:

- ✓ California
- ✓ Connecticut
- ✓ Massachusetts
- ✓ Oregon
- ✓ District of Columbia
- ✓ Vermont

- ✓ New Jersey cities of Bloomfield, East Orange, Irvington, Montclair, Newark, Passaic, Patterson, Trenton, and Jersey City
- ✓ Seattle and Tacoma, Washington
- ✓ New York, New York[1]

Personal leave

Personal leave is time off for personal reasons that are typically not included in sick leave or vacation leave. Personal leave usually amounts to one to three days a year, typically provided on a "use-it-or-lose-it" basis. It's often used for religious observances; that way, employees who feel "forced" to take off Christmas Day don't demand to substitute a different religious holiday (or days).

Bereavement leave

Bereavement (or funeral) leave is paid leave for an employee to attend the funeral of a family member and/or attend to estate-related activities of a deceased family member. The length of bereavement leave is usually "up to three work days," depending on travel time and estate circumstances. Some organizations' policies limit the type of family members for whom employees can take bereavement leave, such as "immediate family" or "children, spouses, and parents." If the relationship to the deceased family member falls outside those limits, employees can usually take paid personal days or vacation time.

Health Insurance

Health insurance (including hospitalization and medical benefits) is probably the most contentious of the core benefits because of the dramatic increase in premium costs. As those increases mount, more small businesses are dropping coverage or, at the least, employees pay a greater portion of the premium—especially for family and dependent coverage.

The Patient Protection and Affordable Care Act, commonly known as the Affordable Care Act (ACA), nicknamed

"Obamacare," is a United States federal statute enacted by the 111th United States Congress and signed into law by President Barack Obama on March 23, 2010. The term "Obamacare" was first used by opponents, then reappropriated by supporters, and eventually used by President Obama himself. Together with the Health Care and Education Reconciliation Act of 2010 amendment, it represents the US health care system's most significant regulatory overhaul and expansion of coverage since the passage of Medicare and Medicaid in 1965.

The ACA's major provisions came into force in 2014. By 2016, the uninsured share of the population had roughly halved, with estimates ranging from twenty million to twenty-four million additional people covered during 2016.

The increased coverage was because of an expansion of Medicaid eligibility and major changes to individual insurance markets. Both involved new spending, funded through a combination of new taxes and cuts to Medicare provider rates. Several Congressional Budget Office reports indicated that these provisions reduced the budget deficit, and that repealing the ACA would increase the deficit. Obamacare also enacted a host of delivery system reforms intended to constrain health care costs and improve quality. After the law went into effect, increases in overall health care spending slowed, including premiums for employer-based insurance plans.

For the most part, the act retains the existing structure of Medicare, Medicaid, and the employer market. However, individual markets were radically overhauled around a three-legged arrangement. Insurers in these markets are made to accept all applicants and charge the same rates regardless of pre-existing conditions or sex. To combat adverse selection, the act mandates that individuals buy insurance and insurers cover a list of "essential health benefits." However, a repeal of the tax mandate, passed as part of the Tax Cuts and Jobs Act of 2017, will become effective in 2019.

To help households between 100 and 400 percent of the Federal Poverty Line afford these compulsory policies, the law provides insurance premium subsidies. Other individual market changes include health marketplaces and risk adjustment programs.

As of this writing in 2018, some states are individually attempting to continue key aspects of the ACA while other states are doing their best to undermine any aspects of the program.

Traditionally, there are three basic types of health insurance plans:

1. Indemnity or traditional plans: Employees can see any physician; physicians receive a fee for service; there are limits on the dollar amount of coverage over time; annual deductibles are common; and the premium is usually more expensive than that for other types of health care plans.

2. HMO: Health Maintenance Organizations restrict the employee's choice of physicians to those specifically in the HMO group; physicians receive a fixed fee per patient or a salary; and cost-control mechanisms are prevalent (use of nurse practitioners to screen patients, and wellness and preventive programs are common).

3. PPO: Preferred Provider Organizations are a blend of traditional and HMO plans; there are contractual arrangements with physicians who agree to fee schedules and other plan requirements; and employees can choose from among more physicians than under the HMO plan but fewer than under the indemnity plan. Employees may, however, be able to see physicians outside the PPO plan network after deductibles and/or with copayments.

Consumer-driven health care plans are a relatively recent type of health insurance that attempts to address the issue of increasing premiums. These plans, known as FSAs (flexible spending accounts), HRAs (health reimbursement accounts), or HSAs (health savings accounts) have two common characteristics: 1) Premiums under a high-deductible health plan are a fraction of those under a conventional health plan. The high-deductible plan does not begin to cover health care costs until the annual deductible (for example, $2,000 individual/$4,000 family) is reached; and 2) concurrently, the employer makes contributions to the designated employee reimbursement, spending, or savings account. Funds in this account meet health care costs until the deductible is reached each year.

In theory, the initial cost of the high-deductible premium plus the contributions to the spending account is no greater than with conventional health insurance, employees are not likely to reach the annual deductible, the funds building in the account are enough to meet expenses, and the account builds significantly from year to year, to the point where little additional contributions are needed to cover the insured adequately.

COBRA

The Consolidated Omnibus Budget Reconciliation Act (COBRA) requires employers with twenty or more employees to provide continued health care coverage to individuals and qualified beneficiaries after termination of employment for up to eighteen to thirty-six months, depending on the circumstances. Employers are required to notify employees who are leaving and their family members of their COBRA right to continued coverage. However, at least 100 percent of the premium must be paid by the former employee. Some states have more generous COBRA provisions.

Life insurance

Employer-provided group life insurance has become a common feature of the employee-benefit package. Most employers provide some level of life insurance. Often, life insurance is "bundled" with another benefit, such as health insurance. Traditionally, group life insurance was considered "burial insurance," so the expected amount was minimal. More recently, expectations have risen significantly, so that the minimal level of coverage is $10,000, with more firms offering one year's pay up to $50,000. Employers can provide up to $50,000 of group life insurance coverage to employees on a nontaxable basis. The value of coverage above $50,000 is considered a taxable benefit to the employee. The $50,000 "ceiling" is a limitation the IRS made years ago so the plan would not discriminate in favor of the more highly paid employees. Since then, salaries have risen significantly, and employers started to provide life insurance worth more than $50,000.

There are two very basic types of life insurance:

1. Permanent life (also known as variable life, whole life, universal life, or yet-to-be named variations) builds a redemption value into the insurance plan. Because permanent life insurance is expensive, few employers provide it.

2. Term insurance is in force for a specific time period, such as five years, fifteen years, and so forth. Employers typically purchase term insurance that covers employees during their employment only, with such policies as, "Life insurance coverage begins the first of the month after date of hire and ends the first of the month after termination of employment."

For an employee group whose age span is representative of the working population, the premium for group term insurance is considerably less than that of life insurance the employees could purchase individually—that is, group term life insurance can be a valuable addition to the core benefits package. And few employees will opt for coverage above $50,000 because they must pay income tax and Social Security tax on the "excess" coverage.

To calculate the IRS's taxable amount of excess insurance coverage, go to the IRS website and search for the uniform premium table. To compare term life premium costs, measure them in cents per $1,000 dollars of monthly coverage. For an employee with a $35,000 life-insurance benefit, for example, if the monthly premium is $4.20, the cost is $0.12 per $1,000.

Accidental Death and Dismemberment (AD&D) insurance is usually an inexpensive add-on (rider) to the basic group-term-life policy. With AD&D coverage, an additional benefit is paid if death is caused by an accident or if the employee loses a limb, eye, or other body part. For a monthly two or three cents per $1,000 of coverage, AD&D can be a very inexpensive compliment to the basic group life insurance coverage. Some insurance policies insist on inclusion of AD&D coverage for all employees with the group-term-life coverage.

Variations on basic group term insurance include, for example, business travel accident coverage, which provides a benefit if the employee is disabled, or if a dismemberment or death occurs, while traveling on company business.

Disability insurance

Disability income insurance provides for the replacement of pay when the employee is unable to work because of illness or disability. Unlike sick time, disability insurance is administered by a third party that determines eligibility and the amount of payment. Although considered a "salary continuation" benefit, typically the benefits paid are less than the employee's salary. There are two general disability insurance plans: short-term and long-term, based on the length of coverage.

Both plans stipulate an "elimination period" during which the employee must be unable to work because of accident or disability. Also, both plans include a length-of-coverage clause that defines the longest period for which a covered employee will receive disability benefits. The extent of coverage defines the amount of benefit the employee is to receive. Typically, the coverage equals 66 percent of the employee's salary, up to a maximum amount per month.

Short-term disability insurance provides a regular income after a shorter elimination period (two weeks to one month), and it lasts for up to three or six months, depending on the policy selected. It typically costs employers more than long-term plans.

As an alternative to purchasing short-term disability insurance, some organizations provide extended sick leave until the long-term disability insurance begins. Others allow employees to purchase their own short-term disability plans through payroll deduction. These plans often have very flexible characteristics (such as elimination period, length of coverage, and amount of coverage) so that an employee can select the plan best suited to their needs.

Long-term disability insurance provides a regular income after a longer elimination period and lasts for years, up to retirement age, depending on the policy selected. It is important to note if the long-term disability policy considered provides coverage so long as the disabled employee is unable to work in their own occupation or any occupation. Many disability policies provide a benefit for only a year or two in the employee's own occupation and then will stop the benefit if the employee is able to work in *any* occupation. The most economical way for employers to provide long-term disability is to do so for all full-time employees.

It is important for businesses to dovetail their disability plans with their sick leave programs to ensure that employees have continued salary replacement coverage.

For example:

	Sick leave	S-T disability	L-T disability
	ten days accrued/year	Begins two weeks after disability	Begins three months after disability
		Ends three months after disability	Ends at retirement age
Pay:	100 percent of days accrued	66 percent of regular pay	66 percent of regular pay

State-mandated disability insurance[3]

A number of states have created disability insurance (DI) benefits for employees who are unable to work because of non-job related situations. Such situations may include injuries, illness, pregnancy, and childbirth. The state program provides a partial wage-replacement plan to help workers in six jurisdictions (as of 2018): California, Hawaii, New Jersey, New York, Puerto Rico, and Rhode Island.

The program's objective is to partially replace wages for workers who are ill or injured off the job and are unable to work. Currently, three states (California, New Jersey, and Rhode Island) offer paid family leave, which allows caring for a domestic partner, child, parent, and other family members.

Employees are eligible for DI if they are unable to perform their job duties for eight consecutive days. The weekly benefit varies by state and disability. The maximum duration of the DI benefit is usually twenty-six weeks except for Rhode Island (thirty weeks) and California (fifty-two weeks). To be eligible, a worker must have paid into the state plan for a minimum of twenty calendar weeks.

Retirement plans

Retirement and pension plans are offered through a wide variety of programs, from simple to complex. In the past, workers stayed with the same employers for their entire career, and "defined benefit" plans evolved. Funded by the employer, these plans promised workers a monthly pension upon retirement—based on a formula that included annual wages, years of service, and age at retirement. The employer chose the investment vehicle, and contributions were based on actuarial valuation of the plan to ensure there would be sufficient funds for retirees.

With our more mobile workforce, in which both the employers and employee careers change more frequently, "defined contribution" plans have become the most popular. These plans establish individual accounts for all participating employees. Employers can contribute to the plan by matching employee contributions, although they are not required to do so. Usually, the employee can choose from among limited investment choices, but the plan's success depends on the amount invested and the financial success of the investments chosen. When the employee leaves the employer, they can usually "roll over" the funds accrued to another qualified retirement plan, keeping them nontaxable until they are withdrawn after retirement.

Whenever an employer makes contributions to a retirement plan, the organization should consider the matter of vesting. Put simply, vesting is owning. If an employer's contributions immediately become 100 percent vested, those funds belong to the employee immediately. But if there is a vesting schedule (for example, retirement funds become vested once an employee has worked for the employer for a certain amount of time, such as five years), the employer's contribution will be returned to the organization if the employee is not vested.

How vesting works

Let's say an employer contributes matching funds of $1 for every $2 employees contribute to their retirement account—but the plan contains a five-year "cliff vesting" clause. An employee takes a job with a different employer. If he or she participated in the retirement plan for four and a half years, the employee did not meet the vesting requirement. Consequently, all of the employer's contributions go back to the employer. The employee keeps the remainder (his or her own contributions, plus any investment gain from the retirement plan).

Now let's say that an employer contributes the same match under its plan, which has a graduated vesting schedule: 50 percent after three years' employment; 75 percent after four years; 100 percent after five years. Again, if the employee takes a job with another employer after four and a half years (but less than five years), he or she is 75 percent vested. Consequently, 25 percent of the employer's contributions goes back to the employer, and the employee keeps the remainder.

For small employers, the most popular retirement plans are 401(k), profit-sharing, savings incentive match plan (SIMPLE), and simplified employee pension plan (SEP).

The Employee Retirement Income Security Act (ERISA) is the most significant legislation that affects retirement plans. By following its rules, employers and employees can take advantage of tax incentives, receive insurance protection covering retirement plans, and be assured of proper record-keeping and communications regarding their plans. Because of ERISA, retirement plans must pass a "fairness test" to ensure that they don't discriminate against lower-paid workers.

Discretionary benefits

Discretionary, or optional, benefits can supplement the provisions of core and government-mandated benefits. The more popular types follow.

Education assistance

Education assistance provides tuition assistance primarily for courses at an accredited college or university and occasionally for courses at trade schools or other entities. Reimbursement, which is usually dependent on a passing grade, may include all or a portion of the cost per credit hour, and the courses may or may not have to be directly related to the employee's job.

Transportation subsidies

Transportation subsidies cover all or part of the cost for employees to take public transportation to and from work, participate in car-pooling, or park their cars at or near work.

Add-on health care benefits

Many organizations' health insurance plans include, at little or no additional cost, a prescription drug discount plan and/or a vision care plan. Dental insurance is usually a stand-alone plan that includes basic preventive procedures (cleaning) and partial reimbursement for other procedures. Employee assistance programs (EAPs) provide confidential family and personal counseling services.

Employee Assistance Program

An employee assistance program (EAP) is an employee benefit programs that assists employees with problems that do or may affect the employee's job performance. Employee problems could include mental or emotional health. Typically EAP services are paid by the employer and provided to the employee at no charge. Often the employer contracts with an EAP provider based on the number of employees and the services provided. The interested employee contacts the EAP provider to receive counseling services of limited duration. Although EAPs are primarily aimed at work-related issues, the range of services could include family finances, marital discord, and/or child care services.

Effective use of EAP can resolve on-the-job performance issues and head off a progressive discipline scenario. EAP should not be viewed as a replacement for corrective discipline but, rather, as an intervention tool that provides the employee with the resources to resolve personal issues that have impacted an employee's work-related issues.

Benefits to the employer could include lower medical costs, reduced absenteeism, and higher productivity.

Flexible benefit plans

Section 125 plans under the Internal Revenue Code (often referred to as "cafeteria plans") allow certain expenses to be paid out as a payroll deduction before taxes are computed or taken out. The work to set up and administer these plans is directly related to how complex they are. In order, from the easiest to the most difficult for the employer:

- ✓ Premium-only plans (POPs), the most basic type of Section 125 plans, allow employees to pay their share of the premium for health and dental coverage with pretax dollars.
- ✓ Flexible spending accounts (FSAs), combined with POPs allow employees to use pre-tax dollars to pay for out-of-pocket health and care expenses that are not covered by insurance. Those expenses can include eyeglasses, child care, prescription drugs, and other non-covered items. FSAs are

best administered by a third party for a monthly fee per participant. That method not only relieves staff of an exacting administrative chore to invest their energy elsewhere; it also ensures confidentiality and responsiveness to the participants.

✓ Full cafeteria plans are more popular in larger organizations. Employees choose from a menu of eligible benefits by using credits the employer gives them at the beginning of the year. For example, an employee can choose to spend more pretax dollars on health insurance and less on disability insurance. Full cafeteria plans take careful thought to set up and considerable communication to explain to employees.

Work/life benefits

A growing trend in the benefits arena is to facilitate employees' achieving a balance between work and personal life. Indirectly, paid days off can add more time for vacation, and sick leave provisions that allow using paid time off to care for an ill family member address the balancing act.

More directly, businesses are slowly adding new benefits that can affect employees' family life. Those benefits include childcare and elder-care assistance, financial and health counseling programs, prepaid legal insurance, casual dress, flexible work options (such as telecommuting, job sharing, and compressed workweeks), group purchasing for auto and homeowners insurance, and on-site personal services (ATM, banking, travel, and dry cleaners). Such nontraditional programs can contribute to employees' quality of life at work and at home.

For some employers, the benefits package is a cornerstone of the total compensation package. For others, benefits represent a nagging expense that keeps rising and rising. Overall, however, the importance of benefits can't be ignored: They represent 30 percent of employers' total compensation costs (the balance going to salaries and wages).[4]

Updated message for managers

Whereas some benefits are required by law, others are provided voluntarily by organizations to bolster their strategies for competition in the marketplace and recruitment. Occasionally, benefits can be structured to encourage positive attendance behavior and provide inexpensive insurance coverage that most employees could not afford otherwise.

With few exceptions, the cost of benefits has increased to become a sizable portion of employee remuneration. Health care benefits, for example, have risen far beyond the rate of inflation, prompting some employers to reduce or drop coverage and others to implement consumer-driven health plans that save significant costs to both the employer and its employees.

Author

Michael Strand has more than thirty-five years of experience administering and teaching employee benefit plans, and implementing and managing compensation programs.

7

COMPENSATION
BY MICHAEL STRAND

*Not everything that can be counted counts, and
not everything that counts can be counted.*

—*Attributed to Albert Einstein, awarded the Nobel Prize in Physics*

Compensation can take many forms: pay, benefits, job satisfaction, camaraderie at work, hope for promotion, and more. For this discussion, the word "compensation" refers only to cash remuneration for work. That can include three components: base pay, incentives, and differentials.

Base pay is the salary or hourly wage. *Incentives* are designed to motivate workers to do more—more quickly, more accurately, and more cooperatively. *Incentives* often are paid as bonuses. *Differentials* are unique pay components related to work time or locations, or other less desirable working conditions. For example, employers often apply a shift differential (such as 10 percent or $1.25 more per hour) for workers on evening or overnight shifts. Differentials are mostly industry-specific conventions, provided by organizations to be competitive with other organizations.

The thrust of this chapter will be on base pay with some commentary on incentives. Employers are continuously striving to provide competitive pay without breaking the bank. After all, for most organizations today, payroll is a major cost of business.

To decide what to pay their employees, organizations need a rational methodology, not a hit-or-miss or trial-and-error approach. What follows is a system for analyzing the marketplace and deriving a reasonably competitive compensation system.

Matching an organization's positions

It is critical to make the best matches of an organization's positions to survey positions. A good match is 70 percent or more of the duties. When the best match is not apparent, there is a compensation technique called "leveling" that may be helpful.

Leveling can be considered when a job on a survey has a similar title but the duties are significantly more or less responsible. To make that assessment, survey descriptions must provide sufficient detail. The following is an example of a leveling problem with an organization's accounting clerk position.

Organization's position: Accounting clerk

Accounting clerk: Performs clerical financial responsibilities relating to accounts receivable and accounts payable. Reviews invoices for appropriate documentation. Prepares bank deposits. Maintains accounting reports, spreadsheets, and the chart of accounts. Three to four years' clerical experience.

SIMILAR POSITIONS FROM THREE DIFFERENT SALARY SURVEYS

✓ Survey #1—Accounting clerk: Handles more complex accounting tasks. May provide some training to junior clerical staff and will have some responsibility for allocating/

checking their work, but will not have a direct supervisory role. Typically has five to seven years of experience and a college diploma or certificate.

✓ Survey #2—Accounting support specialist: Performs a variety of accounting support functions, such as compiling, sorting, and preparing documents and reports; issuing bills and invoices; calculating and verifying debit and credit amounts; and posting transactions to appropriate accounts. Four to five years of experience.

✓ Survey #3—Bookkeeper/Accounting clerk: Performs accounting transactions such as posting to registers and ledgers, account reconciliations, verifying accuracy of accounting documents and codes, preparing vouchers, and journal entries.

Survey #1's accounting clerk appears to be significantly more responsible than the organization's accounting clerk. Survey #2's accounting support specialist appears to be very similar to the organization's accounting clerk. Survey #3's bookkeeper/accounting clerk appears to be very similar to the organization's accounting clerk.

To apply a leveling process, Survey #1's data for accounting clerk would be reduced (possibly 5 to 10 percent). Alternatively, the survey data for that position could be excluded.

No changes to the data for the other two accounting positions would be made.

Competitive positioning

The organization can take one of three compensation approaches to determine how competitive they want to be. Specifically, do they want to pay higher salaries than their competition, lower salaries than their competition, or pay in between (the market rate)?

✓ Market lead strategy: The lead strategy is designed to aggressively set salary rates above the market to improve recruitment and retention. The strategy expects results and places pressure on staff to perform at a high level. Adopting market rates (salary range midpoints at the 75th percentile) are usually characteristic of a lead strategy.

✓ Market lag strategy: The lag strategy happens when the organization does not have the financial resources to devote to salaries or the organization attracts and retains employees through nonmonetary characteristics (nonprofit, charitable, or economically depressed environment).

✓ Meet-the-market strategy: Most organizations follow a meet-the-market strategy in which equilibrium of resources is desired. Compensation should not be too high nor too low. Employees are paid fairly and are expected to perform well. Long-serving staff members, through performance increases, are expected to move up through their pay range to a level comparable to well-paid peers in competitive organizations.

Aging or trending salary data

Salary data becomes old or outdated as soon as it is published. There is an automatic three-month delay imposed by the Department of Justice to avoid antitrust problems. And prior to a survey's completion, considerable time is devoted to compiling and arraying the data. However, by a process of adjusting survey data it can be advanced to the date you select.

For example, let's say you have a salary survey with an effective date of January 1, 2019. But you want to advance the data to a target date eighteen months later: July 1, 2020. You can use the Employment Cost Index (ECI) numbers to multiply the salary data as follows:

✓ The ECI measures changes in the cost of wages on an annual basis. Let's say the ECI is 2.9 percent for Year 2019 and 3.1 percent for Year 2020.

✓ Create an age factor for year 1: One plus the ECI rate = 1.029 (for Year 2019)

✓ Create another age factor for Year 2: One plus the ECI rate = 1.031 (for year 2020)

✓ Multiply the two factors (1.029 and 1.031) to yield 1.0609. Use that age factor (1.0609) for all the survey positions you use from that particular survey, and all survey positions will be aged to July 1, 2020.

✓ If one of the survey averages you want to use is $41,000, then multiplying that figure by 1.0609 yields $43,602.99.

If you are using more than one published salary survey, it is important to develop an age factor for each survey because it is likely the effective date of surveys vary from survey to survey. The target date remains the same but the effective date is usually different.

The ECI is not the only measure that can be used. The Consumer Price Index (CPI) or the WorldatWork annual budget data can be used to age survey data.

For those organizations that cannot afford to purchase salary surveys each year, aging can be effective to cover a number of years. However, the more distant the survey data is, the less reliable it becomes in creating a competitive projected salary rate.

Define the pay range

Sometimes referred to as market pricing, defining the pay range is based on the premise that all workers are being paid fairly. We know this is not completely true; some workers are paid more than their work is worth because supply and demand are not balanced. Other workers are being paid less than their work is worth for discriminatory or traditional reasons. Through market pricing, organizations should define the worth of a position, then assess where a specific employee's pay should be on the pay range.

There are two bases on which to define the pay range: the average pay of all (or most) employees in that position, or the prevalent hiring rate for new employees in that position. With either method, the challenge is obtaining reliable information.

Using the average rate provides better data that will help establish a more accurate pay range. Of the two types of averages, mean and median, the latter is best for salary comparisons because it represents the rate at which half of the salaries are higher and half are lower. Using the median rate minimizes a tendency for very high or very low salaries to skew the average.

The best source for finding the median rate for a given position is a published salary survey. There are a number of organizations that publish salary surveys. Local HR associations, industry-centered associations, and the Society for Human Resource Management can provide excellent sources for published surveys. Published salary surveys can be expensive ($400 to $2,000). Once an organization has identified a salary survey that best matches the characteristics of the organization, it is best to participate by providing salary data on a regular (usually annual) basis. Survey participants typically receive a significant discount when purchasing the survey results.

Good surveys have most of the following characteristics: a brief description of the position (sometimes containing typical qualifications such as education and experience); the mean, median, 25th percentile, and 75th percentile; data grouped by organization size (number of employees or annual revenues); geographic location; type of organization; effective date of the data; and a list of participating organizations.

Average pay information is available on the Internet, but be careful: If the data does not reflect your organization's profile, it is probably unreliable. Online market data for sale will probably be more reliable than free data, but there are no guarantees, which brings us back to published salary surveys. WorldatWork publishes the *Survey Handbook & Directory*, which contains many articles on the use of surveys and survey data, as well as a list of hundreds of published surveys according to type and region.[1]

Unfortunately, conducting your own salary survey may be illegal. Court cases in the early 1990s led the US Department of Justice and the Federal Trade Commission to conclude that salary surveys may violate antitrust laws. Consequently, they created an "antitrust safety zone" for such surveys. Among its requirements are: The survey is managed by an independent third party, the data is more than three months old, and at least five participating organizations are reporting data for the survey. Most important, the survey cannot allow participants to identify the compensation paid by a specific organization.

When gathering survey data, if it is more than six months old, consider raising it by a few percentage points to accommodate the general market trend to increase salaries.

Let's create a hypothetical example. Here is a sample worksheet with the data averages you have gathered from one or more salary surveys.

Administrative Assistant		
PROFILE MATCH	MEAN	MEDIAN
Revenues ($1 to $2.5 million)	$36.5	$35.8
Size (under 25 employees)	$37.1	$36.7
Organization type (financial)	$38.4	$38.5
Location (your city or region)	$38.1	$35.9
Market rate		$36.7

You have gathered the survey averages that best match your organization. You decide to give all four profile characteristics equal weight. The result (an average of the median rates) is the market rate for the administrative assistant position, $36,725 (not rounded. Based on these assumptions, half the administrative assistants in other surveyed organizations in your market and with your organization's profile are paid more than $36,725, and half are paid less.

A pay range defines the maximum and minimum for the position. The range spread is the maximum minus the minimum and then divided by the minimum. To create a pay range from this market rate, know the HR practices regarding pay range spreads for different levels of positions. For entry-level and support positions, the range spread is usually minimal: from 35 percent to 40 percent; for professional positions, from 50 percent to 60 percent. The range spread for supervisory and managerial positions is from 60 percent to 70 percent, and for vice president/executive positions, from 70 percent to 80 percent.

The following table will help us create the pay range.

Pay Range Development Factors (Minimum/Maximum)	
35% = 0.8511/1.1489	60% = 0.7692/1.2308
40% = 0.8333/1.1667	65% = 0.7547/1.2453
45% = 0.8163/1.1837	70% = 0.7407/1.2593
50% = 0.8000/1.2000	75% = 0.7273/1.2727
55% = 0.7844/1.2156	80% = 0.7143/1.2857

We pick the slightly wider range spread of 40 percent for this support position. To define the range, refer to the following steps.

1. Identify the range midpoint or market rate: $36,725.

2. Multiply the midpoint ($36,725) by the lower pay range factor. In this example we want a 40 percent range, so the lower factor is 0.8333. Thus $36,725 x 0.8333 = $30,602.9 = range minimum. Round this amount up to $30,603.

3. Multiply the midpoint ($36,725) by the higher pay range factor: 1.1667 for the 40 percent range. Thus $36,725 x 1.1667 = $42,847.05 = range maximum. Round this amount down to $42,847.

Now we have a range containing a midpoint, grade minimum, and grade maximum. To complete the quartile benchmarks, continue with Step 4 and Step 5.

4. Add the midpoint ($36,725) to the minimum ($30,603), then divide by 2 = $33,664 = top of the first quartile.

5. Add the midpoint ($36,725) to the maximum ($42,847), then divide by 2 = $39,786 = top of the third quartile.

Minimum	1st Quartile	Midpoint	3rd Quartile Maximum	Maximum
2	4	1	5	3
$30,603	$33,664	$36,725	$39,786	$42,847

Now we have *fully* defined the pay range with all the important benchmarks. This range represents your marketplace for the administrative assistant position. It is an appropriate range if you want to meet the going rate. But if you want to exceed the market rate, select a new adjusted market rate between the midpoint and the third quartile (perhaps to $38,255) and recalculate the range following those steps.

Using the pay range

To use the pay range effectively, we need to know what level(s) of in-position experience relate to the range benchmarks. Some (too few) salary surveys provide an average time in position for the individual employees. If we knew that the average time in position for the surveyed administrative assistants was 4.5 years, we could place that comparable experience level at the midpoint ($36,725). We could then use the following guidelines to help us make a salary offer to an applicant.

The organization could expect to pay that midpoint ($36,725) or more to a candidate with at least 4.5 years of direct experience at the same or greater level of responsibility.

For job candidates with less direct experience, a lower offer would be more appropriate:

✓ For a candidate with little or no direct experience at the same level of responsibility, offer closer to the minimum of the range—between $30,603 and halfway to the midpoint (that is, the first quartile) $33,664.

✓ For a candidate with two to four years' direct experience at the same level of responsibility, offer between $33,664 and the midpoint of $36,725.

Although there is no assurance that the candidate will accept an offer within these guidelines, they provide a starting point for negotiation.

The midpoint, or market rate, represents the median within which half the administrative assistants in your market earn more and half earn less. Presumably, those in the first half have more experience than the others. So unless particular circumstances indicate otherwise, there is no rational reason for an organization to offer an "experience level" pay rate to a candidate who does not have at least the average amount of experience. It is also important to differentiate between applicable experience (experience building up to administrative assistant) and comparable experience (experience equal to the position).

Benchmarking positions

You probably will not find salary-survey data for all your positions. Ideally, you will have data on half of them, so you can use those positions for which you have derived market rates as your "benchmark" positions. These positions become points in your organizational hierarchy from which you can assign market rates and midpoints for other positions. Here's an example of how it works:

You have a market rate for an administrative assistant at $36,725. Through the surveys, you also have a market rate for a staff accountant at $43,150. But you have no salary data for widget technician, although you believe (based on qualifications, contributions to the organization's mission, and so forth) it should fall between administrative assistant and staff accountant. Create a table similar to this:

Benchmark Positions	Assigned Positions	Market Rate	Assigned Market Rate
Staff Accountant		$43,150	
	Widget Technician		?
Administrative Assistant		$36,725	

Based on your understanding of the three jobs, should the widget technician earn an amount halfway between the two benchmark positions—*$39,937?* Or should the technician's pay be closer to the staff accountant's market rate, say, $41,543? If you are unsure, work up the pay range for both scenarios and look at the salary of the widget technician to see whether that position's placement on the ranges makes more sense under one circumstance than another.

Pay ranges and formal grades

Developing pay ranges can be very helpful in determining hire offers and assessing employees' pay relative to the marketplace. But the decision to have formal grades based on those ranges varies among organizations. Generally, larger organizations (one hundred employees or more) tend to have a formal grade structure; many smaller organizations (fewer than ten employees) administer an effective compensation system without formal grades.

Salary Compression

The condition of salary compression can be a serious concern that impacts the perception of pay fairness. A classic example is when a hiring supervisor desires to hire a new employee with less job experience into a group of employees with greater experience on the job in that organization. The new employee enters employment at a higher salary rate than the rates of current employees.

Salary compression can occur because:

✓ Salary ranges and employee pay rates have not advanced as much as the market. Employees are underpaid in under-graded positions.

✓ The hiring supervisor is enamored with a candidate with a unique background or skills that would be helpful to the work team.

Salary compression may be addressed in a number of ways:

✓ Provide pay increases (equity increases) to the current staff that reduces or eliminates the compression problem.

✓ Hire the new employee at a higher than desired pay rate with the understanding that the current employees will eventually receive greater longevity or performance in-creases over time.

However compression is addressed, do not assume that pay rates are confidential, and therefore, it is not a problem.

Communicating about pay

Communicating pay decisions can pose a significant challenge: How much is communicated, how much is withheld, and how much of the decision-making process is revealed are judgments of the organization's leaders.

According to WorldatWork's *Market Pricing*: "Pay delivers a strong message. No other area is more important to employees in their relationship with their company. . . . [T]he most financially successful companies are more likely to communicate pay infor-mation to their employees."[2]

At the other extreme is this philosophy, from a switching super-visor at a long-distance-telephone firm: "We know that communi-cation is a problem, but the company is not going to discuss it with the employees."

The right approach to communicating depends on the organization's management style and corporate culture as well as on employee perceptions. Here are some questions from which your organization can create a communication plan that makes sense.

What compensation information is communicated?

Following is a menu of communication information that your organization may or may not want to communicate to employees and appropriate supervisors.

- ✓ Individual employee pay change. Communicate each employee pay increase first to the supervisor and then to the affected employee, along with the reason for the increase. Example: "market adjustment," with an explanation such as, "Effective [date], you will receive an increase in your pay from $XX.xx to $YY.yy. This increase will be a market adjustment based on our recent compensation study."

- ✓ Pay grade/range. If you have a formal pay structure, communicate employees' pay grades or ranges individually. The pay grade, of course, identifies the range minimum and maximum and other benchmarks. Communicating the pay range, however, begs the question, "What happens when my pay reaches the maximum for my range?" Typically, the pay range should increase each year as the pay rates in the job market increase. However, the organization should develop an above-maximum (or "red circle") policy for employees whose pay rates are above the maximum for their ranges.

Is their pay frozen until the position's pay range maximum increases to above their pay? Are they eligible for bonuses only? Are the usual merit or general increases paid in the form of a bonus (one-time payment), thereby not increasing their base pay rate? Are they treated the same as all other employees, receiving full merit and market base pay increases, the first year they are red-circled?

✓ Salary schedule. Many organizations publish their complete pay-range schedule (excluding position titles) for all employees to see, reasoning that employees can easily share each other's pay ranges anyway, so there is no compelling reason to keep it secret.

✓ A position's market rate. Sharing the position's market rate with an employee can be an effective retention tool. It informs the employee of what his or her position pays compared with peers in the marketplace. However, like other compensation information, it may be challenged by employees ("How did you determine this rate?"). Most organizations share the market rate with appropriate supervisory-level employees.

To whom is compensation information communicated?

Timeliness and consistency of message will be key in ensuring that proper communication occurs. For consistency, it is hard to beat communicating the message on paper.

Larger organizations (more than one hundred employees) could decide to share more compensation information with managers and coordinators and rely on them to communicate it to their staffs. However, the risk of delegating communication this way is that not all information is likely to be communicated consistently.

The executive or management team is often involved in reviewing expected pay changes before a final decision is made. Any verbal discussion with employees should supplement written documentation to keep executive staff in the communication loop.

How is compensation information communicated?

Minimally, a memorandum to each employee should identify their current rate, the new rate, the effective date of the increase, and which pay period will reflect the increase. Additionally, it should give the reason(s) for the pay adjustment, such as overall adjustment, merit increase, market adjustment, or equity adjustment.

When does the communication take place?

Compensation communication generally occurs in two stages: 1) to affected executives, managers, and coordinators to obtain feedback, anticipate employee reaction, and make adjustments if necessary; and 2) written and verbal communication to employees directly or through their supervisors.

Compensation philosophy

A compensation philosophy is a statement about how an organization administers compensation. Developing the philosophy is an important initiative to clarify the "why" behind employee pay and create a framework to assure consistency.

The compensation philosophy usually addresses:

- ✓ How the organization manages compensation.
- ✓ What market targets the organization uses to set compensation rates.
- ✓ Guidance in the initial setup and ongoing maintenance of the compensation system.
- ✓ How employee compensation is managed.
- ✓ What total rewards strategy the organization uses.
- ✓ Identification of the framework within which compensation is administered.
- ✓ Defining the organization's competitive strategy.

Incentive pay

Incentive pay is intended to motivate employees by paying for performance that exceeds expectations. Incentives can be structured to address short-term achievements or long-term results. There are three major types of incentives: individual, group, and organization-wide.

Individual incentives may be commissions earned by salespeople or a piece-rate system that measures productivity in a manufacturing plant. In an office environment, incentives may take the form of cash bonuses. Whatever the form, provide the reward as soon after the achievement as practical.

Group incentives can be used when it is impractical to assess individuals' contributions. A popular form of group incentive is gain-sharing, in which the group and the organization share, through a cash bonus, the benefits of the group's productivity above and beyond the standard established.

Organization-wide incentives can include profit-sharing and stock ownership. The organization's exceeding of financial goals may result in bonus payments for all employees. The form of the payment may be flat dollar or a percentage of base pay.

A solid compensation structure is founded on an understanding of the organization's positions (job descriptions), identifying the pay for other positions in the marketplace (salary surveys), using survey data to develop pay ranges (compensation methodology), and using the pay ranges to guide supervisors in hiring practices and managing the pay (performance evaluation and pay-for-performance) of employees.

Updated Message for Managers

There are several ways to compensate employees, but the most important way is *fairly*. In larger organizations, salary ranges, pay grades, and forms of other remuneration for work performed are usually set by top management with input from senior staff and the Finance and Human Resources departments. If your organization doesn't have such a pay plan, you might be charged with creating one for your team. That takes research and arithmetic, not just what "seems" fair.

Good managerial judgment trumps past practices every time: You may have to redress past disparities or determine pay for a newly created position, or even defend the reasons for a raise or bonus. But even without an existing template, creating one is easier than you think. Managers and HR professionals can use existing resources to set up a workable and fair compensation plan.

Author

Michael Strand has more than thirty-five years of experience administering and teaching employee benefit plans, and implementing and managing compensation programs.

8

EMPLOYEE RELATIONS

Write people's accomplishments in stone, and their faults in sand.
—*Benjamin Franklin, American statesman and inventor*

Maintaining an environment that is conducive to work is the foundation of a good employee-relations program.

Although some people use the phrase "employee relations" interchangeably with Human Resources, employee relations is actually a subset of the overall HR function in an organization.

Employee relations refers to the ongoing process of maintaining a productive, equitable, and smoothly functioning workplace—a place where employees do their jobs well, get along with each other, and can depend on the organization to help solve disputes impartially. When it comes to employee relations, your three watchwords should always be "fairness," "consistency," and "communication." And your bible should be the Employee Handbook we discussed in Chapter 3. The more situations you can anticipate—and develop policies for—in your Employee Handbook, the easier it will be to treat employees fairly and consistently when problems arise.

The manager's philosophy

Managers can choose to treat employees in a respectful way or not. However, going the respect route is an HR "best practice" that can yield higher levels of productivity and lower turnover. Plus, it's the right thing to do.

Always ask yourself what your organization can do—or what you can do as a manager—to make sure your employees have everything they need to succeed at their jobs. Do they have a clear understanding of their responsibilities? Do they need a coworker to help them complete their assignments? Or maybe you need to institute a formal mentoring program? Many organizations nowadays are experimenting with something called "reverse mentoring"—asking younger employees to help older executives cope with the demands of new technology, a multigenerational workforce, and rapid changes in the corporate culture. The best time to solve employee problems is always before they begin. So be proactive in making sure employees have the tools, the support, and the workplace environment they need to enjoy their jobs and do them well.

If you truly respect your employees, you'll want to make sure that each one has current, realistic performance objectives and a clear understanding of their job responsibilities. To do that effectively, you'll want to improve your skills as a coach and counselor so you can help your employees succeed.

Remember: Your own success as a manager depends on your ability to get things done and reach your goals through your employees. At the same time, you need to lead, support, and develop your team members, which can be a tough balancing act.

Let's start by making a distinction between a coach and a counselor, and then explore how to help employees make a significant contribution to your organization.

Coach vs. counselor

As *coaches,* managers identify their employees' needs for instruction and direction, usually directly related to their performance or career goals. Coaching is a collaborative approach to improving job-related performance. It relies on mutual, progressive goal-setting, personal feedback, and an ongoing supportive relationship.

Most managers coach because it helps retain employees, shows that they care about their employees as individuals, and builds stronger working relationships.

Managers should be ready to coach when a problem occurs, a new procedure is introduced, a job is changed, and/or a skill gap is identified.

As *counselors,* managers first identify problems that interfere with employees' work performance. In such situations, the manager needs to switch from coaching to counseling mode. Think of this as a process that helps the employee define specifically what behavior he or she needs to change in order to improve his or her performance or resolve a problem.

The manager's goal is to be *both* a good coach and a good counselor, and he or she must have the sensitivity to know which mode to use and when. Generally, coaching should precede counseling.

A good manager who is both a coach and a counselor:

- ✓ Motivates employees to do good work.
- ✓ Reinforces good performance.
- ✓ Encourages employees to stretch.
- ✓ Sets clear expectations.
- ✓ Provides positive feedback on an ongoing basis.
- ✓ Provides constructive feedback on a timely basis.
- ✓ Acknowledges employees' progress toward their goals.

Mantra and models

When it comes to giving both positive and corrective feedback, the manager's mantra should consist of six words: *When you see it, say it!*

It should serve as a constant reminder that you need to be communicating with your employees all the time. Make a habit of giving performance feedback on a frequent, scheduled basis. Mark Twain once said, "I can live for two months on a good compliment." But we believe compliments in the workplace should be much more frequent than that. The same goes for constructive criticism.

To make this concept easier to remember, think of two acronyms: FAST and BEER.

Positive Feedback	Corrective Feedback
F = Frequent	B = Behavior
A = Accurate	E = Effect
S = Specific	E = Expectation
T = Timely	R = Results

Because corrective feedback can be a bit more difficult, let's consider the following example:

Richard is a customer service specialist who handles phone calls from corporate customers who have questions about data and computer networks. His manager monitored seven of Richard's phone calls today, and in four of them, the manager heard him chatting with a coworker while a customer was on the phone. Richard's behavior is unprofessional: It compromises the organization's service to customers; it could cost the organization a valuable customer; and it distracts the other staff working nearby. Richard is expected to focus on the customer and provide stellar service, without exception. He should use his breaks to socialize with colleagues. His manager needs to have a serious conversation with him.

Here's how the manager could give corrective feedback using the BEER acronym as a guide:

Behavior: "Richard, I monitored your calls today and heard you talking with coworkers while customers were on the line—on four different calls."

Effect: "This behavior could cost us customers, and it distracts other employees."

Expectation: "As you know, you're expected to focus on the customer exclusively and have no side conversations."

Result: "You can turn this around. You have the ability to be one of our best customer service representatives if you save your socializing for break time. And I'll be one of your biggest supporters."

Telltale signs of employee problems

An employee who isn't meeting performance expectations might say he or she doesn't know how, or hasn't been provided with the resources needed, to perform a certain task. Perhaps he or she just doesn't *want* to focus on doing the job the right way. This is definitely something the manager should explore.

Many symptoms can indicate performance problems that are likely to get worse instead of better unless you intervene, including:

- ✓ Decreased productivity.
- ✓ Poor quality work.
- ✓ Missed deadlines.
- ✓ Avoidance of tougher tasks.
- ✓ Disorganization.
- ✓ Leaning on others.
- ✓ Being away from the desk for long periods.
- ✓ Upward delegation.
- ✓ Little or no initiative.

✓ Increased complaining.

✓ Lack of cooperation.

✓ Blaming failures on others.

✓ Lack of enthusiasm.

Poor performance can adversely affect your organization in several ways:

✓ Decreased productivity.

✓ Decreased morale.

✓ Customer dissatisfaction.

✓ Increased stress.

✓ Decreased efficiency.

✓ Increased cost.

Clearly, unsatisfactory performance must be identified and corrected on a timely basis.

It benefits us, as managers, to create the type of work environment and communication needed to minimize performance problems. But sometimes, despite our good efforts to correct poor performance, issues remain.

Performance improvement plans

The longer you can keep the communication between you and your employee positive—that is, talking about "improvement" rather than punishment—the better chance you have of turning the situation around. Once you start down the road of discipline, it's hard to get off, and lest we forget, the ultimate destination of that road is termination. That's why it's prudent to start the process with a Performance Improvement Plan, or PIP.

A PIP is a written document designed to help the employee achieve a measurable and acceptable level of improvement. Ideally, it should serve as a kind of roadmap to success by charting a clear course with firm objectives and realistic steps for meeting them. Underperforming employees are often confused and uncertain about what they can do to get better at their jobs. That's where the PIP comes in. A sound written PIP should contain:

- ✓ Clear, accurate details about failing performance.
- ✓ Effects of the situation.
- ✓ Standards that require change.
- ✓ Specific resources and other helpful suggestions.
- ✓ Milestone dates to assess progress in meeting goals.
- ✓ End date by which improvement is expected.
- ✓ Consequences of meeting or not meeting objectives.
- ✓ Employee's signature.[1]

When coaching and counseling aren't enough

If you have made every effort to help an employee, yet significant problems still exist, you must address the situation quickly and firmly, usually following a specific sequence.

Progressive discipline is the manager's effort to be fair and equitable. It provides several opportunities for the employee to improve. But discipline should be initiated only after ensuring that the problem has been investigated (and determined to be legitimate) and sufficiently documented.

Disciplinary options include:

- ✓ Informal discussion.
- ✓ Verbal warning.
- ✓ Written warning.
- ✓ Final warning.
- ✓ Termination.

Before taking these steps, the manager should prepare a complete chronology of specific facts and events. In the initial discussion, the manager should guide the employee to agree that a problem exists. The manager should go over the facts while giving the employee an opportunity to respond or explain. Together, they should plan a remedial course of action in detail—outlining what needs to be done and setting dates for when changes must be made. It's critical for the manager to offer genuine assistance or training, if appropriate, to help the employee succeed. The manager conscientiously monitors the situation, and should acknowledge and reinforce improvement as it occurs.

Once the employee has met expectations, recognize his or her success. If the employee has not met expectations, review your documentation with the HR department or legal counsel to prepare for termination of employment.

Checklist for discussions

✓ Make it private and productive. Arrange a time and a place where you won't be distracted or interrupted.

✓ Create a comfortable and problem-solving atmosphere.

✓ State your purpose clearly:

→ Give your perception of performance against agreed-upon standards.

→ Explore possible contributing factors.

→ Describe what you want, need, or expect from the employee.

✓ Check the employee's understanding of what's expected.

→ Ask for, and listen to, the employee's point of view.

→ Ask questions to understand the context of the actions or behavior at issue.

✓ Identify what changes are needed.

→ Agree on a timetable and a method of measurement.

→ Communicate clearly what happens next if the problem is not resolved.

→ Express support and encouragement.

→ Set up a method for monitoring the employee's progress.

Documentation

To prepare for difficult conversations, managers must make notes as a habit, including both negative and positive performance.

Good performance management entails creating a clear, accurate, written memo shared with the employee that objectively captures the performance issues and the commitments made during the conversation. See pages 114 and 115 for a Sample Memorandum of Warning.

Tips for Effective Documentation

✓ Do not use emotionally charged words.

✓ Focus on the performance or behavior, not the employee.

✓ Be objective and clear.

✓ Clarify performance expectations and the consequences of failure to improve.

✓ Make notes on meetings immediately afterward.

✓ Keep the notes confidential (share only with those who have a need to know).

Termination

"Termination" of employment technically includes both resignation (voluntary) and being laid off or fired (involuntary). When the employer decides on the latter, it's often because of poor performance, misconduct, or changed business needs that require eliminating or restructuring positions. Cases of egregious misconduct may subject an employee to immediate termination; such cases are sometimes referred to as "termination for cause."

Finally, if the poor performance, insubordination, or failure to follow organization policy is not corrected following the last appropriate warning—or there is a relapse after progressive discipline—a manager should consider termination.

Termination is one of the most difficult parts of a manager's job, and the message is one of the hardest for an employee to hear.

Regardless of the reason for a termination, managers should always deliver the news in a sensitive and humane way—and not until they are sure that termination is the appropriate step.

Before deciding to terminate an employee, consider the following questions:

- ✓ Would you take the same step for any employee in this situation?

- ✓ Is this a lawful, nondiscriminatory reason for termination?

- ✓ Have your supervisor(s) or top executives reviewed and approved your decision to terminate?

- ✓ Will you be able to explain the termination decision to the employee clearly and honestly?

- ✓ Will you be able to justify the decision if necessary?

Once the decision is made, use the following step-by-step procedures.

How to Conduct a Termination

BEFORE THE MEETING

- ✓ Prepare a "recommendation to terminate" memo and obtain appropriate approvals.

- ✓ Decide on the amount of severance, if appropriate.

- ✓ Notify colleagues who have a right to know.

- ✓ Schedule a place for a private meeting.

- ✓ Check your state's law to determine whether the meeting needs to include giving the employee a hand-cut check for hours worked since the most recent paycheck.

✓ Invite a representative from the HR or legal department to sit in, or—if those departments don't exist at your organization—invite another senior manager.

✓ It is wise to anticipate a range of reactions from the employee who is being terminated. Remain calm and clear; it can be devastating news.

DURING THE MEETING

✓ Briefly explain the termination decision to the employee. Review progressive disciplinary steps and other measures the organization has taken to help the employee. Be direct and to the point.

✓ Give the employee an opportunity to react and respond.

✓ Clarify that the decision is irreversible and that upper levels of management agree with the decision.

✓ Collect all company property from the employee (such as keys, IDs, passes, or laptops).

✓ Remind the employee of the organization's policy regarding references, if one exists.

✓ Explain the right to apply for unemployment.

✓ Discuss health insurance, the employee's final paycheck, payment for unused vacation, and if appropriate, severance pay.

Sample Memorandum of Warning

Confidential Memorandum

Date: [Current Date]

To: [Employee]

From: [Supervisor, title]

Subject: [Performance concerns]

As we discussed during our meeting of [date], I am concerned about your job performance. Specifically, I have concerns about the poor quality of many of your work products, including written memos and reports. These written products, as I showed you, often contain many grammatical errors, misspellings, and typographical errors.

One of your responsibilities as a [job title] is to be able to "review and proofread outgoing correspondence, checking for proper format, grammar, and punctuation." Some of the examples I shared with you during our conversation included:

X

Y

Z

As a [job title], you are also expected to perform most of your duties without immediate supervisory oversight. In too many instances, I feel I have to provide more guidance than I give others in order to get our department's work completed. A recent example of this was [include specific details].

One of the key factors in our performance appraisal form is quality of work. This factor is critical to your achieving each of the objectives we set together at the beginning of our performance cycle and reconfirmed in our meeting of [date]. At this time, the quality of your work is below the acceptable standards we set during the same meeting at the beginning of our performance cycle.

To help you improve the quality of your work, I will meet with you weekly for the next sixty days. During this time, I will review most of your written work with you. If you need assistance or have questions in between our meetings, I will help you. However, I expect you to work toward completing routine work on time and correctly— the first time.

Please review this memo carefully; it is intended as a corrective action. I expect to see substantial and sustained improvement both during and after the sixty-day period and, if at any time I do not see that level of improvement, we will have more serious conversations up to and including a termination discussion.

Please let me know how else I can help you improve in these areas and whether you have any questions about this memo.

I have read and understand this warning and have had the opportunity to discuss it with my supervisor.

Name
Date

✓ Inform the employee in person or by providing a letter stating that they will receive information regarding benefits, wages, insurance, pension or rollover, and the like by mail.

✓ Get a forwarding address.

✓ Get signature(s) on confidentiality agreements and other applicable forms.

✓ Explain when and how the employee should exit the building.

✓ Explain the policy regarding future access to the office.

✓ Tell the employee that this is a confidential process and will be shared with only those who have a legitimate need to know.

✓ Discuss how you will notify coworkers.

✓ Escort the employee to his or her office or desk area while he or she gathers personal belongings, or offer to pack and mail them. If possible, minimize the number of employees who might be nearby during this step.

✓ Throughout the process, always allow the employee to retain his or her dignity.

AFTER THE MEETING

✓ Share the employee's departure with the work-group in the agreed-upon manner; be sensitive and concise.

✓ Notify appropriate internal staff and any customers, vendors, or other external people affected by the employee's leaving.

✓ Write a summary of the termination meeting. Have the witnesses (HR, legal, other manager present) sign and date that document.

✓ Send checks to the terminated employee (or make sure that finance or HR does so).

✓ Determine who will take over the employee's responsibilities, and if that person is on staff, discuss the work with him or her.

- ✓ Don't make the meeting long.
- ✓ Don't go on the defensive.
- ✓ Don't be insensitive.
- ✓ Don't use humor.
- ✓ Don't make promises you can't keep.

Updated message for managers

Frequent, specific, accurate, and timely feedback is one of the most critical requirements for sustained high-level performance. Without it, performance may fail.

When performance or behavioral issues exist, treat the employee as an adult and provide genuine support for them to change.

In our combined fifty years in the Human Resources field, sometimes we feel like we've seen every kind of performance, behavioral, and disciplinary problem imaginable. Unfortunately, employees keep coming up with new and different ways to require counseling, discipline, and termination. At the time of this writing, some of the hot-button issues in employee relations include sexual harassment, workplace bullying, inappropriate use of social media, transgender bathrooms, and using office Wi-Fi for personal business. That's just a partial list, and we suspect that by the time this book reaches you there will be even more challenges in employee relations.

Your job is to make sure you identify and *anticipate* as many of these issues as possible. Create a legal, non-discriminatory policy for dealing with each of them. Then make sure your employee handbook clearly defines that policy—exactly how you expect your employees to comply with it—and what will happen if they don't. Remember: Your watchwords are *communication, consistency*, and *fairness*. If you get those three things right, you will go a long way to creating a happy and productive workforce.

9

LEGAL CONSIDERATIONS
BY PAUL MICKEY, ESQ.

It is the spirit and not the form of law that keeps justice alive.
—Earl Warren

NOTICE

This chapter summarizes some of the key employment law issues for managers and HR staff. Every employment situation is different and may be covered by a variety of federal, state, and local laws that are beyond the scope of this overview. This chapter is not intended to be, and should not be used as, a substitute for specific legal advice.

The US workplace is subject to a host of federal, state, and local laws aimed at protecting employees. But the prospect of facing a legal challenge should not paralyze managers. Armed with an understanding of the legal framework governing HR, managers can achieve their business objectives with minimal legal risk.

Employment at will

Most managers have heard of "employment at will," but many misunderstand it. The concept of employment at will is still bedrock law in almost every state: An employer can terminate an employee at any time and for any reason (just as the employee can resign at any time and for any reason), provided the reason isn't unlawful. The problem is, the grounds on which a termination (or other adverse action) can be deemed unlawful have proliferated greatly, so as largely to swallow the rule.

Managers need to recognize the gamut of legal challenges they are most likely to encounter, and learn ways to guard against them. Here, we'll review the principal legal issues managers should bear in mind as they hire, manage, and terminate employees.

Hiring

Equal Employment Opportunity (EEO) laws seek to provide equal opportunity to all workers by barring certain specific forms of discrimination against employees and applicants. Retaliation against workers who assert their rights under these laws, or who assist others to do so, is illegal.

Three federal EEO statutes are of cardinal importance:

1. Title VII of the Civil Rights Act of 1964 (Title VII) (applicable to employers of fifteen or more employees) forbids discrimination based on race, color, gender, national origin, or religion. In 2015, the EEOC ruled that discrimination on the basis of sexual orientation or gender identity is a form of prohibited sex discrimination. Additional federal legislation may influence that ruling at some point; meanwhile, many states and cities have already protected workers from discrimination on the same grounds, and company

policies typically track the broader protections available under their state and local law.

2. The Americans with Disabilities Act of 1990 (ADA) (also applicable to employers of fifteen or more employees) bars discrimination because of a person's physical or mental disability, and it requires the employer to provide reasonable accommodations to disabled individuals during the hiring process and during employment, absent undue hardship. The ADA protects those who are actually disabled, who have a record of a disability, and whom the employer regards as disabled.

3. The Age Discrimination in Employment Act of 1967 (ADEA) (applicable to employers of twenty or more employees) prohibits discrimination based on age against employees age forty or over in favor of younger workers. There is no upper age limit, except in very narrowly defined circumstances, so mandatory retirement is illegal in most cases.

BFOQs

EEO law recognizes that certain protected characteristics may be "bona fide occupational qualifications" that an employer can legally consider. For example:

✓ A theater hiring performers for female roles may exclude male applicants from consideration.

✓ A religious institution may require that its clergy share the religious beliefs of the hiring institution.

These BFOQ exceptions are very narrow and unlikely to apply in a typical workplace. Race can never be a BFOQ. And note that "unaccented speech" is not a BFOQ; insisting that an employee be able to speak clearly and comprehensibly is a legitimate business requirement, but declining to hire someone because of a heavy accent is likely to be deemed national origin discrimination.

Do's and don'ts of pre-offer questions

✓ In job advertisements or other recruiting materials, do not imply a preference for applicants of a particular age, race, gender, or other legally protected characteristic.

✓ Do not engage in discriminatory hiring to try to please your customers; customer preference is never a defense to a charge of employment discrimination.

✓ In employment applications or interviews, do not ask questions that will provide information you would be legally barred from using, such as an applicant's age or national origin.

✓ Several states now bar questions about prior salary, and many states and localities have "ban the box" rules prohibiting questions about convictions before a conditional offer is made.

✓ Remember: The ADA imposes very strict limitations on the medical inquiries you can make during the hiring process. Before you offer a job, you can't ask questions that could disclose the existence of a disability. Examples of *prohibited* pre-offer questions include:

→ How many sick days did you take at your last job?

→ Have you ever filed a workers' compensation claim?

→ What medications are you currently taking?

✓ Examples of *permissible* pre-offer questions include:

→ Can you perform this job, with or without reasonable accommodation?

→ Do you need a reasonable accommodation to perform this job? (Ask this one only if you believe the candidate has a disability that would interfere with his or her job performance.)

Drug tests are not considered medical exams for ADA purposes and can be required (subject to applicable state laws) before or after the employer offers the job. More liberal laws governing marijuana use for medical or recreational use make this area tricky in many states, so proceed with caution and good legal advice.

The best way to avoid EEO problems during the hiring process is to make hiring decisions based on a clear definition of the requirements of the position you are trying to fill, not on stereotypical assumptions. Don't pass over the mother of young children because you assume she will be less willing to work long hours. However, feel free to look elsewhere if she tells you during the interview that she must leave work at 4:00 p.m. to collect her children from daycare, and that is incompatible with the job requirements. That's a legitimate business decision based on fact, not on an assumption. Stereotypical assumptions about pregnancy can be a form of sex discrimination and often give rise to legal issues, so proceed with caution and an open mind.

Negligent hiring

To avoid this state-law claim, you must take reasonable care when hiring employees. At the least, you should:

- ✓ Closely review documents applicants have submitted to find any gaps or inconsistencies that they need to explain.
- ✓ Always check references, even if all you learn is "name, rank, and serial number." At least you've confirmed that the applicants stated their work history correctly.

Contract issues

When an employer and a new hire sign a written document entitled "Employment Agreement," the parties will be bound to honor the promises in it. Managers often forget that there are other ways employers can create legally binding contractual obligations. Assurances given during a job interview can be interpreted as binding commitments. If you say, "You'll be a VP by next spring if you take this job," the applicant may take the statement as a promise, and a reason to pass up other job offers. If the position does not materialize as forecast, the angry employee may file a claim for breach of contract. Statements made in offer letters can also be construed as contractually binding, as can statements in a poorly prepared Employee Handbook.

To minimize the risk of inadvertently creating contractual rights, you should:

✓ Understand that what you say to an applicant, verbally or in writing, may be viewed as a binding commitment.

✓ Steer clear of statements that could appear to be guarantees of long tenure, particular disciplinary processes, or career paths, unless you're sure your organization will be able to make good on those assurances.

✓ Include in your employment application form, offer letter, and employee manual a statement that employment is at will, and that the at-will nature of employment can be altered only by a specific written document signed by the CEO or other senior executive.

Background checks

If you are using a third-party service (such as a credit reporting agency) to obtain credit reports, criminal or driving records, or other background information as part of your hiring process, you must comply with the detailed notice and consent requirements of the Fair Credit Reporting Act (FCRA), as well as with any applicable state laws. The FCRA has additional requirements if you plan to deny employment based entirely or in part on the results of the background check. For more information, check the Federal Trade Commission's Website (*www.ftc.gov*).

In addition to the federal requirements under the FCRA, many state laws limit how employers can use criminal records. Generally, using arrest record information is prohibited, and conviction information can be used only if it is relevant to the position being filled.

Immigration

The Immigration Reform and Control Act (IRCA) requires employers to verify all new employees' identity and eligibility to work via Form I-9 within three business days of hire. The form is available at the website of the federal Citizenship and Immigration Services (*www.uscis.gov/files/form/i-9.pdf*).

Some points to remember:

✓ Everyone must complete a Form I-9, whether they were born in the United States or not, within three days of hire.

✓ Form I-9 prescribes which forms of documentation are acceptable; the employer can't require the new hire to produce more or different documents.

✓ If the documents the new hire presents appear genuine, the employer must accept them.

On the job

Remember: The EEO laws ban discrimination in all terms and conditions of employment, including compensation, training, assignments, disciplinary action, and layoffs. Here are some actions that might invite legal challenge:

✓ Reassigning an employee to remedy the problem posed by dating relationships in the chain of command. Changing reporting lines may be the right solution, but be sure there is no suggestion or pattern of gender or other bias in the decision regarding who is reassigned.

✓ Admonishing an employee in their review for complaining about treatment by a strict supervisor. If the employee's complaints include any suggestion of unlawful discrimination, the reprimand could be seen as a signal of retaliation.

✓ Declining to assign an employee who wears a hijab to a position with regular visitor contact. "Customer preference" will not be a legitimate defense to a claim of religious discrimination.

Lawful on-the-job conduct

Several issues have arisen in recent years that might catch even seasoned HR professionals by surprise:

✓ Many states and cities have relaxed restrictions on medical or recreational marijuana, and employer rules that might discipline employees for using or possessing marijuana need to be evaluated and applied taking those laws into account.

✓ States and localities have varying and evolving laws governing the possession of firearms and the places they may lawfully be taken. Again, employers must tailor their rules accordingly.

✓ Social media has had a profound impact on the workplace. Its ubiquity has prompted some employers to impose restrictions on its use in the workplace, and in general, reasonable restrictions on the extent of social media use have been upheld. Employer supervision of the content is a trickier matter. The National Labor Relations Act is primarily relevant to the unionized workplace, but section 7 of the NLRA protects the right of all employees to communicate about the terms and conditions of employment, and provides sanctions for employer attempts to restrict their communications. Employees' online speech about supervisors, pay, and company policies has been held to constitute protected "concerted activity" beyond the employer's control. Company policies governing the use of social media should be crafted carefully with input from counsel familiar with the NLRA.

EEO and independent contractors

Title VII, the ADA, the ADEA, and most state EEO laws protect employees and job applicants, but not independent contractors. The legal line between employees and contractors is not always clear, and employers sometimes find themselves sued for EEO violations by workers designated as "contractors" but claiming to be employees. Consult your legal counsel for advice about the correct classification of those who are providing services to you to lessen the likelihood of being considered a joint employer. (Note: Misclassification of employees as contractors can create serious tax and FLSA problems as well.

Harassment

The prohibition against discrimination also bans harassment based on a legally protected characteristic. Illegal harassment is defined as unwelcome conduct if:

- ✓ Enduring the offensive conduct becomes a condition of continued employment.
- ✓ The conduct is severe or pervasive enough to create a work environment that a reasonable person would consider intimidating, hostile, or abusive.

Some examples of harassing behavior include making fun of an employee's religious beliefs or referring to foreign-born employees using derogatory epithets. The harasser can be the victim's supervisor or coworker, or a nonemployee such as a client or vendor. The victim does not have to be the person directly harassed, but can be an onlooker or anyone affected by the offensive conduct.

The "work environment" is defined broadly for these purposes: unlawful harassment can occur, not only on the employer's premises during work hours, but also wherever and whenever the employee is working for the employer, such as at a client's site, a conference, or even a work-related social event, such as the annual holiday party.

The most familiar type of harassment is sexual harassment. There are two basic types: quid pro quo harassment (seeking to trade job favors for sex) and environmental harassment (creating a work environment that is hostile based on gender). Sexual harassment includes acts such as touching a coworker inappropriately, engaging in derogatory stereotyping about one gender, telling obscene jokes, or displaying pornographic images. The victim can be a man or a woman, and the harasser doesn't have to be of the opposite sex for the conduct to be illegal.

Given the view of the EEOC and the laws under many states and localities—that harassment of LGBT employees is unlawful discrimination—employers should be alert to any harassment based on sexual orientation, gender identity, or the transition of transgender employees.

As a manager, what can you do to minimize the risk of unlawful harassment in your workplace?

✓ Be a positive role model. Avoid engaging in conduct that could reasonably be viewed as harassing.

✓ If you suspect a problem may exist, gently inquire, instead of waiting for it to become serious.

✓ Address inappropriate behavior before it rises to the level of illegality. Your standard of respectful behavior should be higher than what is legally forbidden.

✓ Make sure your organization has a clear written policy prohibiting all types of workplace harassment, and publicize a confidential complaint procedure so that employees know how to report suspected harassment.

✓ Train both supervisors and nonsupervisors about harassment prevention as part of new-hire orientation, and provide refresher courses periodically.

✓ If you receive a complaint of harassment or otherwise become aware of it, move promptly to investigate, and if you decide that the behavior described in the complaint really was harassment or other inappropriate conduct, take meaningful action to remedy the problem immediately.

✓ Handle any harassment investigation with care and discretion so as to avoid legal claims from not only the complaining employee but also the accused harasser or coworkers asked to bear witness.

✓ Ensure that employees who make or support complaints of harassment in good faith do not suffer retaliation.

Protection for sick or disabled employees

A variety of legal rights apply to sick or disabled employees, starting with their entitlement to time off (leave).

The main federal leave law is the Family and Medical Leave Act (FMLA). It applies only to employers with at least fifty employees. To be entitled to FMLA leave, the employee must:

✓ Have been employed by the employer for at least twelve months.

✓ Have worked at least 1,250 hours during the twelve months preceding the leave.

✓ Work at a location where there are fifty or more employees within a seventy-five-mile radius.

The FMLA entitles eligible employees to take twelve weeks of unpaid leave in any twelve-month period for any of these reasons:

✓ Their own serious health condition.

✓ Caring for a spouse, parent, or child with a serious health condition.

✓ The birth of a child to the employee.

✓ Fostering or adopting a child.

An employee may choose, or (in most jurisdictions) the employer may require the employee, to substitute accrued paid vacation, personal leave, or sick leave during this period. Also, leave covered by workers' compensation may count against the employee's FMLA entitlement.

The definition of a "serious health condition" is complex, and it is not the same as a "disability" under the ADA. An ADA disability typically involves a long-term condition, but a serious health condition can be as temporary as the flu, provided the employee: 1) has been unable to work for three consecutive days; 2) has seen a health care provider; and 3) has been prescribed medication. For more information, check the US Department of Labor's website (*www.dol.gov*).

State leave laws

Many states and some cities have enacted their own leave statutes, addressing time off for illness, pregnancy, child-birth, and family care. State workers' compensation laws may also cover employees injured on the job. Check your state's laws to determine which rules apply to your employees.

SOME *FMLA* DO'S AND DON'TS:

✓ Do include an FMLA policy in your employee handbook, and post an FMLA notice in your workplace (available at *www.dol.gov*).

✓ Do give employees taking FMLA leave written notice, within two business days, that their leave will be counted as FMLA leave.

✓ Do remember that the FMLA allows employees in some situations to take intermittent leave in separate blocks of time or on a reduced schedule.

✓ Do reinstate an employee returning within the FMLA leave period to their prior position or one that is virtually identical, unless the employee would have lost their job regardless of the leave.

✓ Don't retaliate against an employee for taking FMLA leave (including a negative performance review criticizing the employee for missing time or falling behind while on FMLA leave).

The ADA

The FMLA is not the only law that entitles employees to take leave for health-related reasons. Granting leave to allow a disabled employee to seek treatment or recuperate can be an accommodation under the ADA. Unlike the FMLA, the ADA doesn't provide for a specific amount of leave. Instead, the employer must decide what is "reasonable" under the circumstances. The answer will depend on many factors, including the employee's position and the likelihood that he or she will be able to return in the foreseeable future. Don't assume that once an employee's FMLA leave has been exhausted, the employer's ADA accommodation obligation has been satisfied, for in some cases, more than twelve weeks of leave will be a reasonable accommodation.

Other ADA accommodations

In addition to time off from work, a disabled employee may be entitled to other reasonable accommodations in order to perform the essential functions of the job, including:

- ✓ Changing a work schedule.
- ✓ Providing adaptive devices (for example, a magnifying reader for a vision-impaired computer user or speech-synthesizing software for a visually impaired employee).
- ✓ Modifying the job by removing nonessential functions.
- ✓ Reassigning the employee to a vacant position that better accommodates his or her disability.
- ✓ Making existing facilities accessible.
- ✓ Providing a reader or interpreter.

The employer is not required to eliminate essential job functions, or to lower quality or production standards, as an accommodation.

If an employee requests an accommodation, how should you respond?

- ✓ Have a direct discussion with the employee, as he or she is often in the best position to know what accommodation will be sufficient and workable.
- ✓ If you were unaware of the disability or don't see a need for an accommodation, you may require the employee to provide documentation to support the accommodation request.

✓ You don't have to provide the precise accommodation the employee seeks if you can provide another effective accommodation.

Substance abuse

Most employers do not tolerate substance abuse in the workplace. Your Employee Handbook should state clear policies regarding drug and alcohol use. You can ban the use or possession of alcohol or illegal substances in your workplace, and forbid employees from coming to work impaired by drugs or alcohol. If your company is a government contractor or federal grant recipient, you may have additional obligations under the Drug Free Workplace Act.

The ADA also addresses substance abuse. Alcoholism is considered a disability for ADA purposes, and rehabilitated drug abusers are protected as well. Current drug addiction and casual drug use are not protected under the ADA. What does this mean for managers?

✓ Alcoholic employees are entitled to reasonable accommodation under the ADA, such as time off to seek treatment. Rehabilitated drug addicts are also entitled to reasonable accommodations.

✓ You can hold these employees to the same standards of performance and behavior as all other employees.

✓ You may not discriminate against alcoholics or rehabilitated drug abusers.

Minimum wage and overtime

The Fair Labor Standards Act (FLSA) establishes a minimum wage of $7.25; many states and localities have higher minimum wages. (An Executive Order sets the rate at $10.35 for federal contractors, and most states have set minimums higher than the federal rate, as have many cities.)

The FLSA also governs overtime pay and requires that any employee who works more than forty hours a week be paid at time and a half for those hours—unless the employee is "exempt." The FSLA definition of "exempt" status centers on the nature of the employee's work and how they are paid. Generally speaking, nonsupervisory employees who perform jobs requiring little independent thought or the exercise of discretion will not be deemed exempt. The nature of the work, and not the job's title, determines whether the employee is exempt or not. For example, though there is an exemption for "executives," an employee in the position of "executive assistant" who spends most of his or her day copying, filing, and typing will not be deemed exempt for FLSA purposes. In most cases, the employee must be salaried (not hourly) to qualify as exempt. The reverse is not true, however: Simply being paid a salary is not enough to make an employee exempt. The FLSA is one of the most complex employment laws, so always consult employment counsel to ensure that your organization is in compliance.

Here are some common ways managers trip over the FLSA:

- ✓ Labeling an employee "exempt" in an effort to recognize the employee's contributions, when the employee doesn't qualify as exempt under the federal regulations.

- ✓ Assuming that everyone who is paid a salary is automatically exempt, regardless of the job's duties.

- ✓ Discouraging non-exempt employees from submitting claims for overtime pay.

- ✓ Giving non-exempt employees compensatory time in a subsequent workweek instead of overtime pay.

- ✓ Docking exempt employees' pay for absences of less than a full day (except for FMLA leave) if the employee has used up all their paid leave.

For more information, check the US Department of Labor's website (*www.dol.gov*).

Retaliation

Title VII and a wide range of other employment laws include explicit prohibitions against retaliation. Courts uniformly uphold the principle that an employee has a right to bring a claim without fear of reprisal, even if the claim is not valid (so long as it is not shown to be in bad faith). Indeed, where an employer takes some adverse action following the filing of a claim, it is not uncommon for the underlying claim to be dismissed and the retaliation claim to succeed.

Managing an incumbent employee who has filed an EEO charge or similar claim is a particular challenge and warrants the involvement of HR and legal expertise. Discipline or other management discussions the employee does not like are not precluded, but the employer must be prepared to justify them clearly, so that a judge or jury concludes they are unrelated to the filing of a claim.

Pay equity

The federal Equal Pay Act prohibits sex-based wage discrimination between men and women in the same workplace who perform jobs that require substantially equal skill, effort, and responsibility under similar working conditions. Because the EPA requires strict comparability between positions, and thus doesn't address many forms of pay inequity, there has been considerable litigation challenging gender-based pay discrimination under Title VII. In recent years many states have adopted more aggressive pay equity statutes, making it easier for women to challenge compensation in relation to that provided to men. A key role of HR is to understand what laws and tests apply, and work with counsel to ensure that risk is minimized.

Termination

The laws described in the last section are the combustible material of employment litigation, but the spark that ignites them is the employee's sense of being treated unfairly or disrespectfully, without forewarning or apparent justification. With remarkable frequency, fired employees will ask, "Why me?" or "Why now?" or "If me, why not her?" If you anticipate those questions and have a record and explanation that addresses them, you will be less likely to face a lawsuit (and more likely to prevail). Here are some key principles for minimizing your legal risk.

Be consistent

Be sure your termination decisions are consistent—that is, don't be exposed to the claim that you treated an employee in a protected category less favorably than employees not in that category. Don't discharge a woman for profanity if men aren't sanctioned for being profane, and don't fire an older worker for repeated tardiness if younger workers are merely given a warning. If you don't have an adequate track record or the demographics to demonstrate that people in different categories are being treated evenhandedly, be sure you have a compelling and nondiscriminatory business reason for your decision.

Be fair

If the termination is because of continued poor performance, make sure you've given the employee clear notice of the problems and a reasonable chance to address them. The employee may surprise you by performing better once a warning is delivered, and if not, you'll be in a stronger position to defend your discharge decision. Private sector, at-will employees are not legally entitled to due process, but judges and juries often sense that all employees should have fair warning and a chance to improve.

Follow procedure

Check your employee handbook and follow any termination procedures in it. Failure to do so could land you with a breach of contract claim or be used as evidence of discriminatory motivation in an EEO suit. If the employee has an employment agreement, make sure you've complied with its termination provisions.

No surprises

Ask yourself whether the employee will be surprised to hear he or she is being let go. If so, consider whether some additional warning would be useful, and ask yourself whether the employee will suspect any ulterior motive. Employees who are caught by surprise often look for an alternative explanation and suspect (or allege) unlawful treatment. Think through your reasons clearly beforehand,

and be prepared to explain them succinctly, to dispel suspicion that improper motives were involved.

Consider requesting a signed release

A properly crafted release agreement, signed by the employee and accompanied by severance pay (or something else of value to which the employee wouldn't otherwise be entitled), will stop an employee from successfully pursuing a claim for damages. The release must be knowing and voluntary to be enforceable—thus you must provide the employee with time to review it and the opportunity to consult counsel. Where claims of age bias are to be released, specific periods to consider the release (twenty-one days for individuals, forty-five for groups) and to rescind it (seven days) are required by statute. Check with counsel when preparing a release agreement.

Pay final wages on time

Most state laws dictate when an employer must pay a departing employee the final paycheck, sometimes including accrued vacation pay. Those deadlines can be tight, so make sure you comply with the rules in your state.

Give neutral references, or be careful what you say

Providing a substantive reference entails some legal risk, particularly if the reference is negative or inaccurate, and it costs the employee job opportunities elsewhere. Overly positive references also raise legal concerns. For that reason, most employers adopt a "name, rank, and serial number" reference policy: They provide only dates of employment and last job title, and they confirm last salary if presented with the figure.

If you prefer to share more information, here are some tips for minimizing risk:

✓ Have a policy that references aren't given unless an employee signs a release.

✓ If a poor performer requests a reference, politely suggest that they ask someone else. You have no obligation to provide a reference, and warning that a testimonial wouldn't be strong is only fair.

✓ If you do get asked for a reference, make sure the person seeking it really is a prospective employer. Ask for the name of the company and then call the person back using that company's main number.

✓ Ask about the nature of the position for which the employee is being considered, and limit your reference to discussing attributes relevant to that position.

✓ Talk about only what you know is true, not what others have said or speculative observations.

Updated message for managers

A host of employment law issues govern your management of human resources. You can't completely eliminate legal risk, but you can minimize the risk that an employee will sue you, and you can greatly improve your odds of prevailing. Here are simple rules for doing so:

✓ Treat employees fairly and consistently, the way you would like to be treated.

✓ Follow your organization's published policies.

✓ Don't base employment decisions on stereotypes or assumption; be in the habit of articulating legitimate, non-discriminatory business reasons, even if just for your own reassurance.

✓ If in doubt, check with an expert in your HR department or your employment counsel.

If you follow these rules, you'll not only minimize your legal risk, but also maximize the likelihood of making sound business decisions.

Author

Paul Mickey has practiced employment law for more than three decades and has held top management positions that have given him firsthand experience in fashioning and implementing challenging personnel decisions. He has handled several leading employment law cases, including the US Supreme Court's first ruling on environmental sexual harassment.

10

MANAGING A DIVERSE WORKFORCE

*Cultural diversity and inclusion thrive when people with
unique perspectives work together to achieve common goals.*
—*Candice Bernhardt*

There's nothing new about diversity in the workplace. In the past we may have thought our organizations appeared homogeneous, but diversity was represented. We've just become a lot more aware of it and realized that having a diverse and inclusive workplace is a really good thing!

In our rapidly changing world, we're increasingly aware that focusing attention on managing a diverse workforce is not just a good idea—it is a business necessity. That attention used to be given to race and gender, but now we also look at diversity in age, ethnicity, physical ability or disability, sexual orientation, religion, and national origin and culture—and those are just the visible elements of diversity. We now need to address the invisible elements, such as:

✓ Diversity of thought.

✓ Work experience.

✓ Education.

✓ Marital/family/parental status.

✓ Religious beliefs.

✓ Socioeconomic status.

✓ Military experience.

✓ Work style.

✓ Communication style.

✓ Geography.

According to Barbara Mitchell and Cornelia Gamlem in *The Essential Workplace Conflict Handbook,*

> *Diversity dimensions aren't the only things that differentiate and shape individuals. Also impacting our behavior are critical cultural dimensions or variables. Culture is the acquired knowledge people use to interpret experiences and generate behavior. Culture is shared by almost all members of social groups and is something older members of the group pass on to younger members. In addition to shaping behavior, culture structures our perceptions of the world—our attitudes, beliefs, and values.[1]*

In today's complex, global environment, workplace diversity is really about creating a respectful, inclusive work environment in which every employee has the opportunity to make a meaningful contribution to the organization's mission and goals.

How can diversity strategies tie into an organization's business objectives? Once the goal of enabling every employee to contribute is reached, the organization is able to:

✓ Attract and retain the best talent.

✓ Reduce the costs of high turnover, absenteeism, and low productivity.

✓ Have greater flexibility and adaptability in the rapidly changing marketplace.

✓ Increase sales and profits.

Establishing a diverse culture

To start, you need to be absolutely sure your organization's leadership supports, and will actively participate in, increasing employee diversity. Without that support, nothing else will succeed. The best way to get top leadership support for diversity and inclusion is to make the case that a culture of diversity has a positive impact on the bottom line.

Once you have the support you need, review the organization's current policies, procedures, and practices to ensure they support diversity. If not, make any necessary changes, get the appropriate approvals, and announce the changes to employees.

Review the organization's website to be sure its diversity-related material is true, useful, and meaningful. Potential clients and job candidates who visit the site want information that will help them determine whether they want to do business with or work for the organization.

Review the organization's Intranet to be sure that the information available for employees states the commitment to diversity and inclusion.

Use representative employee photos and stories on the website and on the Intranet that are natural and authentic. Include men and women of various races, ethnicities, and generations, and people with a visible disability or other aspects of difference—but don't feel compelled to show all dimensions of diversity in every photo, which can detract from the impression of authenticity.

Review the strategic plan and the HR plan to be sure they support diversity and inclusion. If they do not, work with the leadership to make the necessary changes.

The Business Case for Diversity

Why the emphasis on diversity? Diversity is as much a business issue as it is a personal issue. Diversity provides a better return on the investment in human capital by helping to attract and retain the best, brightest, and most creative talent. As the marketplace and your customer base become more diverse, employing a diverse workforce allows you to capitalize on a diverse marketplace.

Traditionally, one of the biggest drivers for diversity has been the changing demographics such as gender, race, and ethnicity. Beyond demographics, there are other factors that contribute to the ever-changing composition of the US population and workforce. These include environmental and cultural factors that differentiate and distinguish us as individuals such as work experience, communication style, education, and generational differences.

Although it is important to understand the demographics, it is equally important to move beyond representation issues and identify issues that create barriers to working effectively and productively with the marketplace. The challenge is to recognize that differences exist, respect those differences, and leverage them for the success of the organization.

—Cornelia Gamlem
President, *The Gems Group*
Author, *The Essential Workplace Conflict Handbook*
and *The Conflict Resolution Phrase*

Inclusion

Diversity and inclusion are frequently lumped together but they aren't the same thing. According to an article in *Harvard Business Review*, "In the context of the workplace, diversity equals representation. Without inclusion, however, the critical connections that attract diverse talent encourage their participation, foster innovation, and lead to business growth won't happen. As noted diversity advocate Vera Myers puts it, 'Diversity is being invited to the party. Inclusion is being asked to dance.'"[2]

Recruiting a diverse workforce

In the knowledge economy, recruiting for diversity is an organizational strategy for business growth.

Top candidates seek organizations that have strong leadership and opportunities for growth. The tougher the labor market is for a particular job, the more effort is required to attract and hire minority candidates. Employers face increasing competition for the best talent—diverse or not.

How can an organization position itself to find and keep the best? Research the websites of firms in your region that do a particularly good job of recruiting diverse candidates to see what they're doing; odds are you will find something you can try yourself.

Some organizations rely heavily on certain sources for job candidates—and those sources may not yield a high number of minority applicants. Review recruiting sources your organization is using to be sure they will bring you the best talent. Look outside the traditional sources. (See "Sources for minority applicants" at the end of this chapter.) If you rely heavily on employee referrals for new hires and your current workforce isn't diverse, you will not increase the diversity in your organization. Review the language in your organization's ads or online job postings to eliminate exclusionary words.

For example, besides recruiting at minority schools, investigate other universities that may have large minority populations. Use employees who personify your organization's current diversity to recruit at job fairs or on campus.

Once you've successfully recruited a minority candidate, the way you introduce him or her to your organization's culture (see Chapter 3) is critical: If your organization has a mentoring program, get your diversity employees into it as early as possible. It is difficult enough for any new hire to merge into a new organization, but there are added challenges for minority employees.

Older workers

Although employers are rethinking their attitudes about older workers, several faulty perceptions persist:

- ✓ Older workers can't learn new skills. Yet people older than fifty are the fastest-growing group of Internet users.

- ✓ Older workers take more time off for illness than younger workers. In reality, attendance is higher among older workers.

- ✓ Older workers cost the organization more money to employ, but such costs as vacation and pensions are usually outweighed by the decrease in recruitment and training expenses because older workers tend to stay with an employer longer.

The AARP developed a National Employer Team in collaboration with companies that appreciate the talent older workers bring to the workplace. AARP serves as a clearinghouse for vetting the employers. Information on the National Employer Team and how firms can apply is available at *www.aarp.org/money/careers/ findingajob/featuredemployers/info.html*.

Some employers have developed phased retirement arrangements for workers who are nearing the end of their careers. These programs benefit both the worker and the organization because they provide a transition for the employee from full-time to part-time work while the organization retains the institutional knowledge, so that the retiring worker can transfer it to others.

Diversity committees and councils

Some employers encourage diversity councils to help facilitate organizational change and put a focus on diversity and inclusion initiatives. These initiatives are intended to increase the demographic diversity and also leverage diversity to maximize productivity.

When selecting people to serve on a diversity council, consider including those who:

- ✓ Have differing viewpoints, so that employees feel their views are being represented on the council.
- ✓ Are adaptable and flexible.
- ✓ Are respected in the organization, so the council's recommendations are credible.
- ✓ Can manage their own biases and be open to listening to others.
- ✓ Are passionate about diversity.
- ✓ Have specific skills the council needs at times.
- ✓ Can view the organization as a whole and see diversity as part of its strategic goals.

Some diversity councils assume certain responsibilities, which can include:

- ✓ Communicating information on affirmative action, cultural diversity, and equal opportunity employment to all employees.
- ✓ Developing diversity policies and guidelines for the workforce.
- ✓ Educating the workforce about issues involving diversity and inclusion.
- ✓ Bringing new diversity-related information to management.
- ✓ Relaying employees' concerns regarding diversity issues to management.

Measuring the impact of diversity

How will you know when you have achieved a diverse and inclusive workplace?

✓ There is a wide range of communication and thinking styles, and everyone is encouraged to share new ideas.

✓ The organization casts a wide net to attract diverse job applicants.

✓ The working environment is friendly and welcoming to everyone, including new employees.

✓ Employees from different cultures share ideas and resources.

✓ Diversity is visible at all levels of the organization.

✓ All organizational materials—including the website, marketing information, and recruitment materials—reflect your workplace's various genders, races, sexual orientations, religions, physical abilities, national origins, ages, and any other dimensions of diversity represented among employees.

✓ There is a commitment to including everyone in the organization—regardless of who they are or where they're from. Everyone has a voice and everyone is heard.

Updated message for managers

Successful managers know that a diverse, inclusive, and engaged workforce gives their organizations a competitive advantage. Managers must actively seek out diverse employees, carefully introduce them into the organization, and use the diversity of thought and experience they bring to maximize organizational effectiveness.

Sources for minority applicants

African-American Career World magazine
http://eop.com

American Jewish World Service
www.ajws.org

The Black Collegian
http://black-collegian.com

Black Enterprise
http://blackenterprise.com

National Black MBA Association
http://www.nbmbaa.org

BlackMBA Magazine
www.nbmaa.org/blackmba-magazine

National Hispanic Business Association
www.nhba.org

Equal Opportunity Publications
http://eop.com

Careers & the Disabled
http://eop.com

LATPRO Hispanic Jobs
www.latpro.com

Project Hired
www.projecthired.org

Diversity Recruiters
www.diversityrecruiters.com

LBGTQ Career Link
www.outandequal.org/;gbt-careerlink/

Transgender Job Bank
www.tjobbank.com

Native American Employment Opportunities
www.nativeamericanjobs.com

Veterans Enterprise
www.veteransenterprise.com

Women's Business Enterprise National Council
www.wbenc.org

Hispanic Job Board Site
www.hispanicdiversity.com/hiring-hispanic/diversity

AfricanAmericanJobsite.com
www.africanamericanjobsite.com

DiversityLink.com
www.diversitylink.com

Diversity Search
www.diversitysearchgroup.com

iHispano.com
http://ihispano.com

Saludos.com
http://saludos.com

Workforce50
Workforce50.com

Quintessential Careers
http://quintcareers.com/mature_jobseekers.html

11

TECHNOLOGY

*Technology is nothing. What's important is that you have
faith in people, that they're basically good and smart, and if
you give them tools, they'll do wonderful things with them.*

—*Steve Jobs*

Imagine you can step into a time machine and visit the office of
a typical Human Resources department fifty years ago. What
would you see?

The first thing you'd notice is all the paper! It's everywhere:
jammed in filing cabinets, stacked on desks, and piled on shelves.
Next you'll hear the constant ringing of telephones. There are calls
from job seekers asking how to apply. Employees are calling to get
answers to questions about their pension or health insurance plan.
A top executive in the C-suite wants to know if they can fire someone or give someone a raise. Every available chair in the office is filled

with job seekers filling out applications. Secretarial candidates are taking typing tests. Nervous employees are steeling themselves for a disciplinary discussion. New hires are eagerly awaiting their orientations.

In the middle of all this chaos, you'll find a harried group of HR managers. Underpaid. Overworked. Unappreciated. They have a reputation for being "cranky" and "mean." But they are actually well-meaning people who are overwhelmed with the day-to-day demands of their jobs. With so many papers to push, rules to follow, laws to obey, and brushfires to extinguish, they rarely have time to think about, let alone participate in, the most important part of their work: finding the best employees and helping them deliver their best performances.

Now take a look at the typical Human Resources department of today—or maybe just a few years into the future—and you'll see a very different picture. Even the name on the office door has changed. It no longer says "Personnel," or even "Human Resources," as it has been for most of the last fifty years. Nowadays, it's more likely to say "Talent Management" or "Human Capital Management."

Inside, you'll find a much cleaner, quieter, and more efficient office. There's hardly any paper or filing cabinets in sight because most HR documents and records are now stored in the cloud. The phone isn't ringing off the hook, because self-service Human Resources software helps employees and managers answer their HR questions and problems from their computers or smartphones. Job seekers, too, can handle much of the application process online—including preliminary screening, skill testing, and even face-to-face video interviews. By the time a job seeker shows up at the office in person, an HR manager knows he or she is one of the top candidates for the position.

Does all this sound like the HR equivalent of some science-fiction novel? It's not. In fact, all of the new technologies needed to bring the typical Human Resources department into the 21st century are either here now or will be in a few short years. The question, then, is simply: Is your organization willing to make the commitment of time, money, and effort to bring these technologies into your office and learn to use them effectively?

HR technology in the 21st century

What follows is a brief overview of the new technologies that are currently revolutionizing the HR profession. With all the choices available, they may make you feel like a kid in a candy store. *But don't give yourself a stomachache!* Remember: Each new technology comes with a price tag, a learning curve, and the inevitable glitches that could make your employees and colleagues wonder if you were better off doing it the old-fashioned way. It's up to you to decide which technologies could improve the way you work forever—and which could cause more problems than they're worth.

Streamline recruiting online

Nowhere is the impact of new technology felt more powerfully than in the area of recruiting. Before the Internet, hiring new employees was a labor-intensive, time-consuming, and money-draining task that involved writing and paying for newspaper ads, reviewing thousands of incoming résumés, interviewing dozens of candidates, and winnowing them down to a precious few—only to find out the hiring manager didn't like any of your choices. And that meant starting all over again!

Thanks to the Internet and especially social media, much of this process can be automated or at least streamlined. With job-hunting sites like *Indeed.com*, you can post a job opening at little or no cost and have it seen by millions of candidates at once. Or you can use social media sites like Facebook or LinkedIn to find the sought-after "passive" job seeker. When the résumés start flowing in, prescreening software can scan for key words and phrases that will help you eliminate hundreds of unqualified applicants and focus on the best candidates. Other kinds of software can test these candidates for their skills, knowledge, and even psychological factors, such as leadership qualities and the ability to work on a team. You can conduct preliminary interviews online with video conferencing technology, saving time and money for both the applicant and your organization. Of course, you'll still need to meet candidates face to face at some point. But by then you'll only deal with the cream of the crop. According to HR technology expert Meghan Biro, browsing online for great talent will be like shopping for shoes![1]

Better decisions with big data

With the help of today's high-speed computers and sophisticated software, we are collecting more data about our employees and prospective employees than ever before. This information helps HR managers make personnel decisions based on actual facts rather than gut instincts or guesswork. It's possible nowadays, for example, for HR to identify teams that are struggling with their assignments and provide the kind of training they need to succeed.

Big data can notify you when employee turnover is becoming unacceptably high in a given department, and if analyzed correctly, it can also tell you why. It won't be long before wearable technology, video surveillance, and even heat-and-motion sensors can tell you who is working and who is not. Of course, the collection of big data raises important questions about privacy in the workplace—questions that must be addressed by new employee policies. More about those in a moment, but first let's look at what happened to all that paper.

The paperless HR office

Human Resources departments have always been heavy users of paper. With government regulations, tax forms, job applications, résumés, payroll records, insurance documents, 401(k) statements, employee contact information, and performance reviews, the typical HR department not only handles a ton of paperwork, but it also needs to store and maintain that paper for long periods of time. Sometimes forever.

That's why HR managers were among the first to embrace the new technologies of electronic imaging and cloud storage. With documents converted into digital formats and stored in the cloud, HR managers can now print the documents they need only when and if they need them—thereby eliminating the time-consuming process of digging through filing cabinets in search of a missing sheet of paper. Legal compliance no longer requires mounds of paperwork. Employee data can be searched by key words in a matter of seconds. If you need a government form, you can download it instantly from the Internet. Best of all, this information can be kept on a tiny computer chip instead of in rows of filing cabinets or at a remote warehouse that sends you a bill each month for storage.

When it comes to security, however, there is both good and bad news. It's much more difficult nowadays for a single disgruntled employee to sneak into HR and get a look at their own (or someone else's) personnel file. But it's easier than ever for a hacker to get into *all* of your personnel files and release them to the public. That's why HR managers must work closely with the organization's IT department to make sure sensitive personnel, payroll, and health records are secure.

Telecommuting and the remote workforce

Who doesn't like to work at home? Just about all of us could use a day out of the office from time to time to focus on our work without phone calls, meetings, and interruptions. For some people, working at home full time is a dream come true. Surveys show that nearly two-thirds of millennials want to work at home full time or occasionally.[2] Thanks to new technology, telecommuting is easier than ever before. But is it a good thing?

The benefits are considerable, both to the employee and the organization. Telecommuting makes it easier to recruit and retain talented employees. The organization saves money on real estate and office space. Employees tend to be more engaged with their work, which results in improved productivity. And telecommuting is socially responsible because it reduces pollution and traffic congestion.

But there are downsides to telecommuting, too. For example: You probably never thought you'd miss office politics, gossip, and water-cooler conversation until suddenly it isn't there anymore. Work-at-home employees sometimes feel forgotten, ignored, and passed over for raises and promotions. They also feel like they're "owned" by the organization and never away from the job because the computer is always calling to them from the next room.

Telecommuting also causes problems back at the office. Mid-level supervisors are even more likely than upper management to resist the idea of telecommuting. Top executives can see the economic benefits, but supervisors only see the problems. How do I make sure people are doing their jobs? How do I track my employees' hours? How can I make sure I'm being fair when I decide who gets to work at home and who doesn't? It's up to the HR department to sort out these vexing issues and provide the training to supervise remote employees effectively. But one thing is for sure: We're going to be seeing more telecommuting, not less, in the years ahead.

Self-service Human Resources

As more and more of the traditional HR functions become computerized and automated, it will be possible for employees and managers to take care of routine HR work by themselves. The Human Resources department, in other words, could become like the self-checkout line at the supermarket! Here are just a few of the HR transactions that can be done by managers and employees on their own:

- ✓ Employee personal data and updates.
- ✓ Employee onboarding.
- ✓ Benefits enrollment.
- ✓ Employee training and e-learning.
- ✓ Performance management.
- ✓ Time and attendance records.
- ✓ Access to handbooks and other policies.
- ✓ Organizational culture information.
- ✓ Wellness surveys and resources.[3]

The benefits of employee self-service (ESS) and manager self-service (MSS) are obvious—lower costs, improved productivity, and higher rates of employee satisfaction, to name a few. As an employee, you will no longer have to call the HR department every time you have a question about your paycheck, your health benefits, or your 401(k). All of this information will be readily available online through a secure portal.

As a manager, you'll no longer need to contact HR for help with such routine management tasks as handling transfers, granting leave, giving promotions and merit increases, or dealing with employees who voluntarily leave their jobs. Compensation and benefits information will no longer be locked up at the HR department and require assistance from an HR manager to view.

ESS and MSS are a win-win for everyone, according to HR technology expert Meghan Biro. "Employees have everything they want at their fingertips. And the burden on HR teams in terms of capturing, updating, and monitoring this information is greatly reduced."[4]

Real-time performance reviews

As we discussed in Chapter 5, the annual performance appraisal has been falling out of favor in recent years. For many reasons, the traditional performance review process was unpleasant for both employees and managers, so it was frequently postponed—sometimes indefinitely.

The advent of new technology, however, has made it easier for supervisors and HR managers to monitor performance on a real-time basis using metrics to make sure employees are meeting agreed-upon standards. Computer technology helps solicit regular feedback from employees to help managers do a better job, too.

And instead of saving all this for one painful meeting at the end of the year that everyone dreads, new software programs have made it possible to create a performance review process that is not only continuous but also more transparent than ever before. These programs use key performance indicators to identify areas in which an employee needs improvement and provide immediate training wherever it's necessary.

"With the integration of technology into the equation," says Meghan Biro, "learning and improvement can be an ongoing process instead of something done just once a year. That's better for employees, better for the teams they are a part of, and also exponentially more expeditious for the HR pros managing the performance management process."[5]

Do-it-yourself training and education

With the rapid developments taking place today in virtual reality, augmented reality, and machine learning, we are quickly reaching the point at which employee training and onboarding will consist of someone handing over a headset and saying, "Strap this on and teach yourself."

According to Jay Samit, author of the bestselling book *Disrupt You!,* there are four key ways that augmented reality and virtual reality could change corporate training forever.

First, virtual reality provides real-time information when it's needed. "A maintenance worker," for example, "could look at a specific make or model of high-voltage equipment on an oil rig and be safely taken through the diagnostic and repair procedure." Second, it will allow supervisors to see exactly what their employees are looking at and give instant advice on how to solve a problem or take advantage of an opportunity. Third, artificial intelligence systems can watch what experienced and skilled employees are doing and bank that information for use by new employees who come along later. Finally, all of these training tools (and more) won't have to wait for the development of new hardware systems. Most of them can be put into inexpensive "apps" operated on the employee's own smartphone.[6]

Mobile and wearable technology

Speaking of smartphone apps and strapping on a virtual-reality headset, the new HR technology headed our way will not only be highly mobile, but much of it will be *wearable.* Today's employees are already accustomed to wearing identification badges around their necks. Imagine if those ID badges were actually miniature computers complete with built-in video cameras, microphones, speakers, a Wi-Fi connection, and enough processing power to provide the answer to any question the employee may encounter during the workday.

The possibilities boggle the mind. But it poses problems, too. One has only to think about the enormous impact that wearable video cameras have had on police work in recent years to realize it's a double-edged sword. On the one hand, wearable technology will help employees stay connected, improve communication, and increase productivity, security, and efficiency. On the other hand, it will be like having your supervisor breathing down your neck all day long!

Social media for employee engagement

We've already touched on the role of social media for recruiting new employees and vetting their backgrounds. But social media also has a role to play in employee engagement. Social media will become a prime source for helping organizations reach their goals because they can use it to tell their success stories through photos and blog posts, Tumblr, and Pinterest pages.[7]

The savvy HR department of the future, in other words, will use various social media platforms to boost employee morale, get employees excited about the organization's success stories, keep them abreast of new opportunities, encourage teamwork and idea-sharing, and help bridge the communication gap between the various "silos" that often exist in a large organization.

There is a downside to social media, however, especially when it comes to your employee's personal use of Facebook, Twitter, and similar applications. Employees who are given free rein to say whatever they want about your organization on Facebook, for example, can inadvertently (or intentionally) do irreparable harm to the organization's reputation, reveal trade secrets, libel their fellow employees, anger competitors, trigger disciplinary discussions, and create all sorts of mayhem for the HR department to handle.

Benefits of new technology in HR

By now it should be clear that these new technologies will bring many benefits to the field of Human Resources management, such as:

More staff loyalty.

Enhanced employee engagement.

Real-time assessment of performance.

Improved employee experience.

Better talent management and recruitment.

Less paperwork and more streamlined bureaucratic functions.

Employees empowered to become better decision-makers.

The elimination of "silos" and improvement of intra-organizational communication.

HR's ability to analyze performance data and thereby offer more customized training.

HR taking on a more strategic role in the organization.[8]

But all of these "pros" come with a set of "cons," too. And many of these will have to be handled with new policies and a substantially revised Employee Handbook.

New technologies require new policies

Your Employee Handbook will have to be revised and updated to make sure all of these new technologies are used and not abused by both employees and managers. Employees have rights when it comes to new technology, but they have responsibilities, as does management. Leaving these matters to chance by not spelling them out in your employee handbook or other official documents could open the door to lawsuits, charges of discrimination, regulatory fines, and even criminal prosecution. Each of these new technologies raises interesting—and perhaps vexing—policy questions. For example:

✓ Who owns an employee's email?

✓ What kinds of websites are appropriate to view on the employer's time or using the employer's equipment?

✓ If your employer has provided you with a smartphone or a computer to use for telecommuting, how much personal use is appropriate?

✓ Can your employer monitor everything you do or say online?[9]

At a minimum, you will need to develop policies for handling emails, smartphones, instant messaging, blogging, social media, personal use of computers, and telecommuting. Joining the Society for Human Resource Management (SHRM) can be helpful in this regard because they provide you with boilerplate employee policies that have been vetted by attorneys. (Although, it's always a good idea to have your own attorney review your policies.) You can also search the Internet to find real policies from large corporations with thousands of employees that routinely deal with a wide range of human behavior and misbehavior. For example, here are a few of the key points made in IBM's policy on social media and blogging:

✓ Make it clear you're speaking for yourself and not for the organization.

✓ Never reveal proprietary information.

✓ Never mention other employees or clients by name without their approval.

✓ Never use ethnic slurs, personal insults, or obscenity.

✓ Don't pick fights.

✓ Always speak in the first person and be honest about who you are.

✓ Steer clear of inflammatory topics like politics, religion, and sex.[10]

The Society for Human Resource Management boilerplate policy adds these "do's" and "don'ts":

✓ Never post internal documents or information.

✓ Don't use your employer's time for social media unless it's allowed by policy.

✓ Don't register on a social media site using your business email address.

✓ Never use social media as a way to retaliate against a supervisor, coworker, or client.

Meanwhile, you should always assert your organization's property rights when it comes to the use of equipment, software, and systems. Don't forget to remind the employee of the organization's right (and responsibility) to monitor their use of email, computers, and the Internet.[11] Of course, every employee policy should end with a gentle but firm reminder that any violation will lead to disciplinary action up to and including termination. In other words, this is serious business.

But don't create draconian policies that completely ban the use of popular technology such as, "No personal use of cell phones at work" because they will be honored more in the breach than the observance. By doing so, you'll create widespread disrespect and disregard for your Employee Handbook. Instead, it's a good idea to acknowledge that certain technologies have become an important part of our lives and should be used judiciously. Think of your policy as a way to *assist* your employees in making responsible, ethical, intelligent decisions about their use of technology.

When enforcing employee policies, the three most important principles are consistency, fairness, and nondiscrimination. If you fire an hourly wage employee in the mailroom for personal use of email, for example, you'd better be ready to fire your executive vice president for doing the same thing. Keep that in mind when you're writing the policy so it doesn't come back to bite you later.

Human resources information systems

The key to making all of these new technologies work seamlessly in your organization is a state-of-the-art Human Resources Information System (HRIS). If your organization does not use HRIS software yet—or if your system is out of date—the following suggestions will help you select a vendor and implement a system that will meet your needs and help you incorporate all the new technologies discussed in this chapter.

Selecting an HRIS program is complex and time-consuming, but it's time well spent given the long-term implications for the organization. Begin by looking at the aspects of your business that drive your organization to implement a new system, and determine how an HRIS will support your overall requirements. This may involve meeting with senior leaders and others to identify what they need from HR.

Next, determine the specifics of those requirements: Are you looking for a system that includes job-applicant tracking, or are you more focused on training records, or the administration of government-mandated programs such as HIPAA or COBRA? Will your employees be comfortable with self-service applications (accessing information about benefits, for example) rather than calling or visiting HR staff? An employer's desire to reduce costs, however, may outweigh the employees' preferences for more personalized attention.

When planning and choosing an HRIS, involving the organization's IT department is crucial: Should you use a standalone PC, networked client/server, or mainframe system? What operating system will it run—Windows, Apple, UNIX, or something else? Does the organization already have computer and software systems with which the HRIS must interface?

Once those questions are answered, document the requirements as specifically as possible so you can choose the right vendor. If it's difficult to clarify goals and requirements at this point, now may not be the right time to move forward. Wait until those are clear so as not to waste time and other resources.

Before seeking vendors, determine how much the organization is willing to spend on software, hardware, and implementation—and develop a budget. This might be hard to do before even talking to vendors, but you should at least have a ballpark figure in mind. Software costs include licensing fees, database licenses, and maintenance. Hardware includes servers, PCs, laptops, and network upgrades. Implementation costs include training, consulting services from the vendor, and data entry.

One final step before approaching vendors: Determine whether or not your own IT department has the ability and capacity to build a system that will meet your requirements. Having IT build your system has many advantages, but it can be time-consuming and divert your technical staff from more pressing assignments. So be sure to ask how quickly the work can be accomplished.

The best way to find vendors is to network with others in your field and ask what systems they use. The Society for Human Resource Management (SHRM) has buyers' guides on its website, which is a good place to start finding potential vendors. Once you have identified some, request product information.

The next step is to prepare a request for proposal (RFP) or a simpler request for information (RFI). It should provide information about your organization and a link to your website, your requirements for an HRIS, and technical specifications, as well as ask for pricing and references. Finally, your request should seek information on customer support and training, plus a sample of the vendor's contract terms.

When you receive the vendors' responses to the RFP or RFI, create a spreadsheet so you can easily compare them and decide which three or four vendors to invite for a product demonstration. In your invitation, specify what software products you want the vendors to demonstrate.

Before each demonstration, assemble a list of questions to ask the vendor. Be sure that everyone involved in the decision can attend the demos, especially the IT staff, whose questions will be different from those asked by management or HR. After the demonstration, ask all attending staff members for their opinions, so that you can list the positives and negatives of each product. Check references and, if possible, visit the references' offices to see the product in action. Meet with each finalist to review once more the programs' features, costs, customer service, product support, and implementation plans. Get everything in writing. Then make your decision!

Does all this sound a bit overwhelming? It's not easy, but you also have the option of hiring an independent consultant to shepherd you through the entire process, offering helpful advice and suggestions along the way. When it comes to something as important as installing a new HRIS system, we think that it is worth the money.

Updated message for managers

With all the new technology in the pipeline, HR managers will finally have the time and tools to focus on the most vital aspects of their work—recruiting talented employees and giving them the training, benefits, compensation, support, and motivation they need to succeed.

As a result of these changes, upper management will no longer look at Human Resources as a back-office *cost* center but as a strategic *profit* center. In today's postindustrial economy, every enlightened CEO knows that their organization's most valuable capital asset walks in the door every morning and out every night. This is why Human Resources will finally have a seat at the boardroom table!

12

TODAY'S WORKPLACE CHALLENGES

There are many ways of going forward, but only one way of standing still.
—*Franklin D. Roosevelt*

It's quite obvious that the world has not been standing still, though sometimes we wish it would! The modern workplace is evolutionary, with resources—human and otherwise—in a state of constant flux. How organizations adapt and react can mean the difference between success and failure.

Workforce changes

The workplace has changed significantly, and the pace of change isn't slowing down. The events and actions of our global economy allow formerly remote parts of the world to have a real impact on US business. We've moved into the knowledge economy, too: The service industry has replaced manufacturing as the core US enterprise.

Work that used to be done here is being "outsourced" to countries that pay lower wages. Technology is changing how and where we work. Employees are seeking a balance between their work and personal lives.

Business ethics

It is recommended that organizations have a written ethics statement that is published and posted around your workplace, then following that code of ethics; discussing your code of ethics in the orientation process; conducting mandatory, annual ethics training for everyone; informing employees on how to report an ethics violation and ensuring that those who report them are not subject to retaliation; setting up a confidential hotline for reporting ethics violations; and continuing discussion of ethics in staff meetings. See page 169 for more information on ethics.

Organizational culture

Each organization, whether for profit or nonprofit, has its own unique culture that flows from the vision of its leaders but also from all the different experiences employees bring to the workplace. Culture also includes the values, norms, systems, language, and assumptions the organization uses to manage staff. Simply put, it's the way things are done in an organization.

Culture has become increasingly important to today's organizations. Prospective employees are encouraged to try and understand the culture before applying for a job or before accepting a new position. This is because they need to know whether they will be able to work in the culture. Hiring managers also evaluate whether or not a job candidate will be a "fit" (see Chapter 2).

Leaders should understand their roles in maintaining or evolving an organization's culture. Leaders are vital to the creation and communication of culture; they are often the principal architects of organizational culture.

Organizational culture is not stagnant and although changing culture isn't easy, it can be done. Many employees resist change, so when change is needed, leaders must communicate the "why" behind the change and not just the "how."

Employee engagement

As Mitchell and Gamlem reported in *The Big Book of HR*, "Leaders everywhere are focused on increasing the engagement of their employees. Increasingly we're seeing that employees, especially Millennials, get bored easily with their work and start looking for some new challenge to spark their interest."[1]

A disengaged worker is potentially unhappy with their assignment or just putting in time—and some people are so totally disengaged that they are busy acting out their unhappiness by undermining what your organization wants to accomplish.

Keeping employees engaged takes some effort but it can be done. It all starts in the hiring process; therefore, be sure that anyone who interacts with applicants is fully engaged and enthusiastic about your organization and the work you do. New-hire orientation is also key to engagement. This is the time when your new hire is excited about the new job and you want to keep it that way by carefully bringing him or her into your organization so that he or she understands the role and the value he or she brings to you (see Chapter 3).

Generations at work

Because people are living longer and working longer, we currently have five generations able to work at the same time in the same workplace. The Millennial generation has now replaced the Baby Boomers as the largest generation, and it's not unusual to have younger people managing an older generation, which can lead to difficulties on both sides.

The impact the generational differences have on the workplace can be a challenge for HR as well as anyone who manages people. What's important is to acknowledge the value each generation brings to the workplace. HR can help organizations deal with the conflicts that arise by employing conflict management skills. A good resource for you is *The Essential Workplace Conflict Handbook*.

A survey by AARP/Roper Starch Worldwide Inc., found that almost 80 percent of Baby Boomers plan to work at least part-time after retirement.[2]

This trend affects organizations on several levels:

- ✓ Boomers aren't retiring, which blocks promotions for younger workers.

- ✓ Employers with older workers may experience higher health care costs.

- ✓ Leave policies (sick and vacation) may need revamping to provide more flexibility in situations where the Family and Medical Leave Act doesn't apply.

As Generation X and Millennials take on significant leadership roles in organizations, work/life balance and workplace flexibility may rival health insurance and retirement benefits to become the top concerns of employees, and the American workplace will be changed forever.

Millennials are more optimistic and entrepreneurial than previous generations. This generation's sense of entitlement will be a challenge for managers. Millennials (those born from 1978 to 1990) want to be entertained, and they are creative, innovative,

Code of Ethics

Among the elements of workplace issues and behavior that a code of ethics might cover are:

Applicable laws.

Confidential or proprietary material.

Conflicts of interest.

Organizational assets or property.

Acceptance of gifts, gratuities, and entertainment.

Privacy issues.

Dealing with the media.

Reporting ethics violations, including a nonretaliation statement.

and resourceful. They don't understand what the world was like before laptops, email, and text messaging.

Generation Z consists of those born after 2000. We're just learning what's important to them at work, but suffice it to say that if Millennials were good with technology, Gen Zers can run circles around Millennials!

Although there are differences among the generations, all of us want the same things at work:

✓ Respect.

✓ Fair treatment.

✓ Equality.

✓ Balance.

✓ Flexibility.

✓ Feedback.

✓ Job enhancement and advancement opportunities.[3]

Let's look at each of the five generations at work.

Veterans (born before 1946)

They expected to build a career with one employer or perhaps in a single field with a small number of employers. Smart organizations are asking Veterans to stay or return to work as trainers or recruiters, where they are able to share their experiences and leave a legacy.

Some positives of the Veteran generation:

✓ Dependable.

✓ Detail oriented.

✓ Thorough.

✓ Loyal.

✓ Hardworking.

Some challenges they face:

✓ Don't like ambiguity or change.

✓ Reluctant to "make waves."

✓ Averse to conflict.

✓ Don't like to discuss feelings.

Baby Boomers (1946–1964)

They have always wanted to excel in their careers, and many have already reached the point of considering what to do with the rest of their lives. Smart organizations are looking for projects that will engage Boomers so their intellectual capital doesn't walk out the door.

Some positives of the Baby Boom generation:

✓ Optimistic.

✓ Driven.

✓ Go the extra mile.

✓ Team players.

✓ Want to please others.

✓ Good at building relationships.

Some challenges they face:

✓ Self-centered.

✓ Judgmental.

✓ Averse to conflict.

Generation X (1965–1977)

Their approach to work is fundamentally different from that of their seniors because many in this generation were "latchkey kids" and learned self-reliance at an early age. Therefore, they will not tolerate being micromanaged, and they need to give and receive frequent feedback. They saw their parents go through downsizings and layoffs, so they don't put much trust in organizational loyalty or job security.

Some positives of Generation X:

✓ Adaptable.

✓ Tech savvy.

✓ Self-reliant.

✓ Not intimidated by authority.

✓ Creative.

✓ Informal.

✓ Pragmatic.

Some challenges they face:

✓ Impatience.

✓ Lack people skills.

✓ Cynical.

✓ Consider work "just a job."

Millennials (1978–1990)

They have heard from an early age that they need to build portfolios to get into the right college to land the right job. They are used to doing many things at once and are so technologically savvy that their families and friends use them as tech support; Millennials must be "connected" at all times. They will probably have several careers in very different fields, so retaining this generation will be a challenge for employers. However, if their organizations offer development opportunities, they may stay a little longer. This generation is the most socially conscious of any since the 1960s.

Some positives of the Millennial generation:

✓ Like structure.

✓ Optimistic.

✓ Self-confident.

✓ Goal oriented.

✓ Inclusive.

✓ Multitaskers.

✓ Tech savvy.

Some challenges they face:

✓ Need structure.

✓ Inexperienced.

✓ Need constant feedback.

✓ Entitlement mentality.

Generation Z (Born after 1990)

This generation says they prefer face-to-face communication with managers rather than using email or even instant messaging. Many Zers say they'd like to someday own their own businesses, and many say they aspire to be leaders. It should be no surprise that this generation wants to work either in the technology industry or with technology. Generation Z employees want to have an impact on the world. People in this generation are very confident that they will be in managerial roles within five years of starting to work.

Some positives of Generation Z are:

✓ Global perspective.

✓ Extremely tech savvy.

✓ Leadership potential.

✓ Highly motivated.

Some challenges they face:

✓ Being managed by others.

✓ Lack of patience.

✓ Overconfidence.

Five Generations

Veterans: Born 1922–1945
Influenced by:
- ✓ Charles Lindbergh's 1927 flight across the Atlantic Ocean.
- ✓ Stock market crash of 1929.
- ✓ Social Security established in 1934.
- ✓ World War II.
- ✓ Hiroshima.

Baby Boomers: Born 1946–1964
Influenced by:
- ✓ Civil Rights movement.
- ✓ Space exploration.
- ✓ Vietnam War.
- ✓ Assassinations of John F. Kennedy, Bobby Kennedy, and Martin Luther King Jr.

Generation X: Born 1965–1977
Influenced by:
- ✓ Watergate.
- ✓ Introduction of the personal computer in 1981.
- ✓ Stock market crash of 1987.
- ✓ Gulf War.

Millennial Generation: Born 1978–1990
Influenced by:
- ✓ Oklahoma City bombing in 1995.
- ✓ Columbine massacre in 1999.
- ✓ September 11th attacks in 2001.
- ✓ Email and instant messaging.

Generation Z: Born after 1990
Influenced by:
- ✓ Global warming.
- ✓ Global focus.
- ✓ Arab Spring
- ✓ Wiki-leaks

Work/life balance

Most people in the workforce want a full and balanced life, but it is only in recent years that they have asked for it.

Work/life balance is a concept that supports the desires and the efforts of staffers to split their time and energy between work and the other very important aspects of their personal lives. It's a daily effort to make time for family, friends, community, spirituality, health, and personal growth while devoting time and effort to the demands of the workplace.

Savvy employers create a work environment in which work/life balance is expected and is supported. Responding to employees' needs for work/life balance enhances the organization's ability to compete in today's ever increasingly competitive labor market. Applicants make decisions based on whether or not an organization supports work/life balance. A healthy balance also increases the odds that organizations can retain outstanding employees who might otherwise leave you in search of balance in their lives.

Employers, too, are looking for greater flexibility—to compete in the global economy. That has created a trend toward alternative staffing arrangements, including hiring independent contractors rather than full-time employees, or maintaining an "on-call" workforce for peak periods. These types of arrangements help employers avoid a cycle of hires and layoffs as they respond to market forces.

Employees are already beginning to see themselves as "free agents" whose skills matter more than where they work. Many now present themselves as available for work on a project-by-project basis, and many organizations bring laid-off employees back as independent contractors. This decreases organizations' fixed-salary and benefits costs while the work still gets done.

To implement alternative staffing, employers must first determine which functions are "core" to the business (for example, those that bring in revenue) and work hard to retain the employees who perform them, then design a structure that accommodates the use of independent contractors, part-timers, or seasonal workers for other positions.

Another approach employers can use is to institute flextime, establishing core business hours when all employees must be present.

Employees work with their managers to determine their own work hours. This allows for such needs as childcare and medical appointments. This avoids the problem of employees having to ask for time off—or being late or leaving early—and their managers know when to expect them on the job.

Daycare and doctor visits aren't the only reasons employees want flexibility. Older workers may want to ease into retirement, adult children may need time to care for elderly parents, and other employees might want to train for an athletic event or volunteer for a favorite charity. Today's fathers often want the same work/life balance and scheduling options as working mothers, yet may fear being stigmatized if and when they use flex benefits.

The generation currently entering the workforce is more likely than older ones to request and expect alternative work arrangements, whether it is telecommuting from home one day a week or working a compressed week. This new generation of workers calls for a different way to determine how productivity is measured, especially when "face time" is no longer an adequate way to judge whether an employee is doing a good job.

All these strategies can have a positive impact on employees and the level of their engagement at work. Each organization should determine what is important to its workforce and then design plans to address issues of work/life balance, telework, and flextime. One size does *not* fit all.

Virtual Workforce

"Work is what you do—not where you go," says John Edwards of Telework Consortiums, based in Leesburg, Virginia.

Pros and Cons of Virtual Workers

Pros

✓ Lower real estate investment. Organizations may be able to decrease their office spaces. Some allocate the same space to several employees, who use it at different times.

Although coordination is needed to ensure adequate work space for each day, this is extremely cost-effective.

✓ Increased productivity. Employees working from home typically have fewer distractions (such as drop-in visits from coworkers) than those working onsite. Productivity can also increase as employees spend less time commuting, allowing more time to work.

✓ Reduced sick leave costs. When employees can work from home, they don't use sick days as often as when they must go to the work site.

✓ Reduced health care costs. If employees can work from home with a minor illness, health care costs may decrease because fewer colds and viruses will spread through the office.

✓ Increased labor pool. Making employers attractive to semi-retired workers, homemakers, and people who cannot commute brings in new talent and helps retain highly valued employees.

✓ Expanded customer service. Employees can serve customers after normal business hours or when the central office is closed for emergencies such as inclement weather and natural disasters.

CONS

✓ Some managers find it difficult to manage employees they can't see, and therefore may be less likely to promote deserving virtual workers.

✓ The cost of technology to support can be high.

✓ Because some positions don't lend themselves to virtual work, morale problems can surface between employees who can and those who can't work virtually due to the nature of their job responsibilities (such as the receptionist or maintenance worker).

An organization that decides to implement a virtual work program should first:

- ✓ Obtain senior management support.
- ✓ Determine what new technology resources will be required.
- ✓ Develop guidelines for the program.
- ✓ Determine which positions (not people!) will be eligible.
- ✓ Develop a strategy to announce the program to all employees.
- ✓ Train managers and virtual workers.

Organizations like WeWork are springing up around the world. In this arrangement, entrepreneurs and freelancers cowork in upscale, shared office space. Members can rent an office or a desk, or have a contract that says they can come in anytime and be guaranteed a desk and be part of a business community.

Outsourcing

Outsourcing Human Resources has gained popularity with companies that can't afford or don't want to hire an extra person or a team for particular functions such as payroll or benefits administration.

The most frequently outsourced HR functions are:

401(k) administration.

Pre-employment testing/assessment.

Background screening.

Flexible spending account administration.

Employee assistance programs.

Health care benefits and COBRA administration.

Temporary staffing.

Pension benefits administration.

Retirement benefits administration.

Relocation.

Payroll.

Retirement planning.[4]

Advantages

- ✓ HR staff can be more strategic. If routine tasks are outsourced, HR can focus on tasks that have more impact on the organization's bottom line.
- ✓ Compliance issues. Vendors that specialize in the legal aspects of HR matters can provide the information required for the company to comply with applicable laws.
- ✓ Efficiency. If the outsourcing firm specializes in a particular area, it should be able to do as much work as company staff, in less time.

Disadvantages

- ✓ Employer privacy. Some organizations don't want outside vendors to know significant aspects of their business.
- ✓ Employee reaction. Current employees may feel less connected to the organization if personal issues such as benefits or salaries are outsourced.
- ✓ Employee relations. Companies that provide outsourcing may not handle such issues as sensitively as on-staff HR professionals. This could create issues that require the organization to step in and handle sticky situations.

Outsourcing Checklist for Employers

In deciding whether to outsource, an organization should consider the following questions:

✓ What do we spend on the tasks we may want to outsource?

✓ How would outsourcing impact our current workforce, especially if it entails eliminating positions?

✓ Who will coordinate with the outsourcing firm, and how will doing so affect that employee's workload?

✓ What criteria should we use in choosing an outsourcing firm? For example, do we want to hire a firm that would keep outsourced functions in this country, or one that could or would send the functions offshore?

✓ What could the remaining HR staff accomplish if routine tasks were outsourced? How much more strategic could we be?

Globalization

Customers are all over the world. So are many employees. Some organizations have offices around the world, and others are owned by foreign investors with headquarters on other continents.

Today's managers need to stay up-to-date on world events and the global economy to work with customers and employees in other countries, and evaluate whether such events will affect the organization's business or employee base. They need training in managing across frontiers.

Employees on foreign assignment should be trained in cross-cultural communication, cultural adaptability, and the language of the assigned country.

Wellness programs

With health care costs skyrocketing, the most effective strategy for cost containment is to promote a healthy lifestyle through behavioral change.

Smoking is the leading cause of preventable death in the United States. The second leading cause is obesity, which increases the risk of developing at least thirty serious medical conditions, and is associated with increases in deaths from all causes.

Managers should consider supporting a wellness program in their organizations. A well designed wellness program can increase productivity, boost morale, and reduce stress. Wellness programs can help employees make smart and healthy choices that potentially reduce health care costs, increase vitality, and cut down on absenteeism.

Tips for a Successful Wellness Program

- ✓ Involve employees' family members in your wellness program.
- ✓ Sponsor health screenings at the workplace.
- ✓ Provide incentives for employees to stop smoking.
- ✓ Encourage participation in the program with incentives after finding out which ones might work with your employees.
- ✓ Consider weight-loss programs such as Weight Watchers at Work.
- ✓ If there is no health club at the office, subsidize membership at a local club through payroll deduction.
- ✓ Reduce stress by offering chair massages at a discount one day a week.

The opioid crisis

The opioid crisis is having an impact on organizations' health care costs as well as their ability to hire employees in areas of the United States where the crisis is the greatest. Although we might think that most people who are struggling with drug dependences are out of the workforce, that simply isn't the case—many people who are drug dependent are working full time.

When employees misuse opioids and other substances, this can negatively impact productivity, drive up disability and workers' compensation costs, and increase absenteeism.

HR professionals need to walk a fine line between compassion and action; this is a place where your employee assistance program provider can give you highly valuable insights and needed help.

It's a good idea to use your "all-hands meetings" to share information on the support that is available and to reiterate your organization's policies on drug usage. Use every means of communication you have to get the word out about the seriousness of this issue.

Addressing opioid addiction can be overwhelming to many managers and others in your organization. Focus on your overall business goals while being sensitive to the needs of employees struggling with addiction. Don't forget the impact this has on your overall workers who have to pick up the slack for coworkers who are absent.

Marijuana in the workplace

With the expanding legalization of medical cannabis and adult-use recreational marijuana, organizations need to reevaluate drug testing policies and marijuana use during work hours. Although the organization has an obligation to maintain a safe work environment, we now need to comply with these new laws and regulations. Employers have the right to install and administer a drug-free workplace policy, which can include limiting the use of marijuana during work hours or the appearance for work under the influence of marijuana (just like they do for alcohol use during work hours).

If your organization has employees in states that have legalized possession and use of medical marijuana and/or adult-use marijuana, you may need a policy with some flexibility. Contact your labor attorney for the best advice as you draft your policies and procedures, and be sure your employees are informed of any policy change (see Chapter 9).

HR analytics

HR analytics is the application of a methodology and integrated process for improving the quality of decisions made around people issues. Although HR analytics relies on statistical tools and analysis, its power lies in the quality of the data it uses.

HR used to rely on anecdotal information to make policy decisions. For example, a senior executive hears an employee in the cafeteria complaining that his or her benefits program is less than stellar. The executive later asks his assistant for an opinion and hears the same story: "Our benefits program isn't any good!" So, at the next leadership team meeting, it comes up for discussion and HR is told to upgrade the benefits package—which might not be needed at all.

Think about it: No one in finance or marketing would ever suggest taking action without lots of research, charts, and graphs to support their recommendation, so why shouldn't HR do the same? Keep in mind that every decision should be tied to the return on investment (ROI). Gather enough data to make an informed decision.

This shift to being data driven is uncomfortable for some HR professionals, but we need to move past those insecurities and increase our knowledge and use of data. This may require taking classes or asking for help from your CFO, but it is essential to adding value to your organization.

HR metrics

The data that HR uses to make decisions should originate from metrics for which measurements are collected, including:

- ✓ Time to fill positions.
- ✓ Cost per hire.
- ✓ Turnover in Year 1/turnover by department/overall turnover.
- ✓ Time until promotion.
- ✓ Revenue per employee.
- ✓ Number of people available for promotion.
- ✓ Billable hours per employee.
- ✓ Employee engagement statistics.
- ✓ Ratio of HR professionals to employees.
- ✓ Effectiveness of HRIS.
- ✓ Absenteeism.

This list is just a start; however, using metrics is critical to the success of the HR function. Facts add credibility, and credibility contributes to your personal success as a HR professional.

Data security

Data or cyber security has become a huge issue for anyone in business today and it is especially important that HR professionals are up to date on how to protect employee data. HR and IT need to partner up to ensure that employee data, which includes highly confidential information, is not susceptible to the ever-increasing data breaches that have impacted so many organizations.

Your IT department should keep you up to date on best practices, but you also should educate yourself so that you can ask the right questions. Your employees need to be aware of your policies on data security and follow them to the letter! It is recommended that data security policies and processes be a part of your new hire onboarding process and updated frequently so your employees and your organization are protected.

An article in the *Huffington Post* entitled "Data Security Must be a Top Priority for HR," suggests that HR professionals must be proactive and understand that "technology (and the potential for breaches) has entered every facet of business today."[5]

Updated message for managers

Managing people seems to entail new challenges at every turn. Managers need to be aware of current events to stay ahead of new trends and issues. To take their organizations forward to the future, they should:

- ✓ Develop a code of ethics and monitor compliance with it.
- ✓ Create a positive organizational culture.
- ✓ Work to maximize employee engagement.
- ✓ Maximize the positive aspects to minimize the differences among generations in the workforce.
- ✓ Create opportunities for employees to have work/life balance and flexibility.
- ✓ Allow for telecommuting and other flexible work options.
- ✓ Carefully evaluate whether outsourcing will benefit the organization.
- ✓ Provide training on cross-cultural issues for both managers and employees.
- ✓ Carefully monitor issues relating to the opioid crisis and its impact on employees.
- ✓ Update policies and practices regarding medical marijuana and adult-use marijuana and get up-to-date guidance from a labor attorney.
- ✓ Make decisions based on data.
- ✓ Partner with IT on data security for your organization and be proactive!

APPENDIX: ADDITIONAL RESOURCES

All forms included in this appendix are samples only. In light of changing legal requirements and state law variations, employers should always consult with employment counsel before using them.

Offer Letter

Dear   :

This letter confirms your discussion regarding employment by XYZ Organization as [Position Title] in the [Name of Department] effective [date]. Your initial salary will be at the biweekly rate of $ [$ if annualized]. There will be a six-month initial evaluation of your performance.

If these terms reflect your understanding of the discussion, please sign both copies, retaining one for your files and returning the other to the Human Resources Department [or manager] no later than [date]. If your understanding is different from the above, please contact me immediately.

Enclosed is your orientation schedule. You will meet with various XYZ Organization staff to discuss payroll procedures and XYZ Organization and departmental policies and procedures. Please take a moment to review the Immigration Reform and Control Act information enclosed and bring the necessary documents with you on your first day. The Immigration and Naturalization Service requires you to present the documents necessary for us to complete our paperwork within three business days of your employment. Your position offer is contingent on your ability to produce the necessary documents within the three-day period.

This offer letter and any other XYZ Organization documents are not contracts of employment, meaning that any individual who is hired may voluntarily leave employment upon proper notice, and may be terminated at any time and for any reason.

We are pleased that you have decided to join our staff, and we are sure that you will enjoy your association with XYZ Organization.

Sincerely,
Jane Smith
Director, Human Resources

Understood and agreed:

John Smith

Sample Job Description

Job descriptions serve as a useful management tool for understanding the role of the support staff, the hiring and placing of applicants, establishing salary structure, and for setting guidelines for promotions and transfers.

Office Manager/Executive Assistant

POSITION SUMMARY

The Office Manager/Executive Assistant is responsible for the sound management of all day-to-day operational functions. Provides administrative and secretarial support to the president. Develops and administers human resources and coordinates with controller. Oversees administration programs and processes designed to attract, retain, and motivate employees. Plans and carries out policies relating to all phases of human resources and administration activities.

The work involves a broad range of related activities that the Office Manager/Executive Assistant must direct and manage in terms of the stated scope and specification of all office activity. The Office Manager/Executive Assistant is expected to exercise considerable independent judgment and decision-making to resolve unusual or complex matters in a manner that is consistent with the preference of the president. The incumbent reports to and may seek direction from the president, but maintains full and direct accountability for final results. The incumbent regularly communicates with the president and coordinates with him on planning.

ESSENTIAL FUNCTIONS

- ✓ Analyzes and organizes office operations and procedures.
- ✓ Implements day-to-day human resources matters including: recruiting, orientation, training, performance evaluation, attendance, and benefits administration.
- ✓ Maximizes office productivity through proficient use of appropriate software applications.

- ✓ Formulates procedures for systematic retention, protection, retrieval, transfer, and disposal of records.
- ✓ Types correspondence for the President, including handling of confidential information.
- ✓ Provides administrative support for the President to include telephone coverage, mail, and necessary communications internally and externally.
- ✓ Assists the President in the management of his schedule.
- ✓ Plans office layout.
- ✓ Maintains personnel records to ensure completeness, accuracy, and timeliness.
- ✓ Coordinates activities of various workers within department.
- ✓ Maintains contact with employees and outside vendors. Serves as administrative liaison.
- ✓ Investigates employee concerns.
- ✓ Manages all activities related to the maintenance of the facilities, office equipment, and systems.
- ✓ Performs special projects as assigned by the President.

REQUIRED EXPERIENCE AND TRAINING

The position requires ten-plus years of general office management experience or any equivalent combination of experience and training that provides the required knowledge, skills, and abilities.

KNOWLEDGE AND SKILL REQUIREMENTS

- ✓ Advanced knowledge of practices, processes, and principles of office management.
- ✓ Knowledge of all standard operating procedures, policies, and procedures.
- ✓ Technologically competent, including working knowledge of Windows, Word, Excel, Outlook, and QuickBooks.
- ✓ Skill and ability to manage multiple/parallel projects.

✓ Skill and ability to take initiative and work under extreme pressures.

✓ Skill and ability to effectively organize/prioritize work and manage time in order to meet deadlines.

✓ Skill and ability to analyze and solve complex problems.

✓ Skill and ability to effectively communicate orally and in writing. Ability to respond to common inquiries or complaints.

✓ Skill and ability to interact with employees, external customers, contractors, subcontractors, third-party consultants, and vendors in an effective and professional manner.

✓ Ability to deliver superior customer service.

✓ Ability to establish harmonious and effective working relationships.

✓ Ability to be discreet and diplomatic.

✓ Demonstrated success in the leading and managing of people.

✓ Ability to interface well with all departments of the organization and to represent the president in a highly professional manner.

✓ Ability to maintain the highest level of confidentiality.

SPECIAL WORKING CONDITIONS

This position may require extended periods of standing, sitting, as well as some repetitive movements and repetitive lifting of minimal weight.

Reasonable accommodations may be made to enable individuals with disabilities to perform the essential functions.

Employee File Checklist

_____Employment Application/Resume

_____Offer/Confirmation Letter

_____Personnel Data Form/Emergency Contact Information

_____New Hire Form

_____Tax Forms

_____Employee Photograph

_____Acknowledgement Form, Receipt of Employee Handbook

_____Acknowledgement Form, Electronic Mail, and Internet Access Policy

_____Time and Attendance Policy

_____Employee Change Notices

_____Performance Evaluations

_____Supervisor's Reports, Other Disciplinary Notices

_____Leave of Absence Request

_____Employment Termination Notice/Resignation Letter

_____Exit Interview

New Employee Questionnaire

Congratulations on completing three months of employment with us. Now that you have become acquainted with the organization, please complete this questionnaire and return it to your manager. Your responses are very important to us. You are not required to sign your name, but listing your department will be helpful.

Was the position you applied for clearly explained during the interview process?

How would you rate the on-the-job training your received?

How would you rate the orientation?

How would you rate the responsiveness of other departments?

How would you rate the communication in your department?

How are the general working conditions in your department?

Is your position what you expected it to be?

Employee Name/Date/Department Signature:

Performance Improvement Plan

Confidential Memorandum

Date:[Current date]
To: [Employee]
From: [Manager] [Title]
Subject: Performance Improvement Plan

On [date], we met to discuss your performance. During this meeting, I informed you that your performance rating for the annual evaluation cycle was Below Standards. I also showed you examples of where your work product didn't meet the agreed-upon standards. As indicated in your year-end evaluation, you required improvement in quantity of work, organizing and prioritizing assignments, and customer service skills, all of which are important components/performance factors in your work for our organization.

In order to help you improve your performance in the areas noted above, I developed the following Performance Improvement Plan [PIP]. Your performance improvement period will begin on [date] and end on [date]. I would like you to schedule an hour with me every two weeks to discuss your progress toward the milestones listed below. I would also like you to document your progress in writing so we can use this information as talking points at our bimonthly meetings.

A Fully Successful level of performance will include the satisfactory accomplishment and demonstration of the following performance factors:

Quantity of work

Due to constant revisions because of incomplete and incorrect final reports, the lag in workflow is impeding the work of our department.

Submit draft reports to me to ensure that they are complete and error-free before finalizing.

Organizing and prioritizing assignments

Handling multiple tasks simultaneously is an important job responsibility. Finding efficient ways to manage your work can prevent important projects from slipping through the cracks. For example, when you did not follow up to clarify the time for the food delivery for our reception, it was not delivered in a timely manner, causing a disruption in our event.

PERFORMANCE EXPECTATION

- ✓ Work closely with other administrative staff to explore different methods of accomplishing tasks.
- ✓ Seek clarity by asking questions when you are unsure of assignment specifications.
- ✓ Manage vendor commitments.

Customer service

Providing lead telephone reception for the department is a very visible responsibility that delivers a critical first impression of our association. Timely fulfillment of member/client requests and prompt responses to telephone inquiries have suffered greatly in the past two months. For example, members often indicated that they have not received requested items and materials from you. It is essential that you answer the phone in a prompt and courteous manner, responding to requests within twenty-four hours.

PERFORMANCE EXPECTATION

- ✓ Answer the phone in a prompt and courteous manner, responding to requests within twenty-four hours.

The previous information represents the expectations that I have of you in your role here. Please know that I am available to assist you in improving your performance in the areas previously outlined.

I look forward to working with you during these next few weeks. Again, I am available to answer any questions you may have or to provide you with any guidance you may require to improve your job performance. However, you should be aware that if you do not improve your performance to a Fully Successful level by [date], or if you have not completed the outlined assignments within the specified time frames and according to the expectations given, I will consider additional measures to address continued performance concerns, which may include recommending termination of your employment. Please let me know if you have any questions or concerns.

I have read and understand this PIP, and I have had the opportunity to discuss it with my supervisor. I understand that termination is a possible consequence if I do not meet and sustain the expectations contained in this Performance Improvement Plan.

Employee's Signature/Date

Sample Warning Memorandums

Confidential Memorandum

Date: [Current date]
To: [Employee]
From: [Manager] [Title]
Subject: Performance Problems

The intent of this memorandum is to follow up on our conversation of [date of most recent counseling] regarding [describe performance/conduct problem[s]], and to ensure that you understand [Organization name]'s expectations going forward.

As you know, we have had several discussions regarding this issue, on [dates of prior discussions]. [Briefly summarize what was discussed in counseling discussions prior to most recent counseling, what has occurred since the last counseling discussion, and the negative impact of the employee's behavior.] In those discussions, I shared with you my concern about your pattern of late arrivals to work. Despite those discussions, you have continued to arrive at work between fifteen and thirty minutes late on average two or three times a week. Your late arrivals impose an extra burden on your coworkers and have a negative impact on the efficiency of our operations.

When we met on [date of most recent counseling], I emphasized to you that it is critical that you [make performance/conduct expectations clear; for example, "Arrive to work at your scheduled start time unless you have received prior authorization from your supervisor to arrive at a later time." If you fail to meet this requirement, you will be subject to serious disciplinary consequences, up to and including termination of your employment with [organization name].

[Employee's first name], I'd like very much to help you succeed at your job here, and I hope that you are able to meet these expectations of your job. If you have any suggestions for how I can help you to improve in this area, I would be happy to discuss them with you.

I would also like to remind you of the resources that are available to you as a [organization name] employee. [List contact info that might be relevant given nature of employee's performance/conduct issues, Employee Assistance Program, Human Resources Department, and so on.]

I have read this warning and have had the opportunity to discuss it with my manager. I understand that my failure to comply with the expectations it contains will be grounds for serious disciplinary action, up to and including termination of my employment.

Manager's Signature/Date

Employee's Signature/Date

Sample Memorandum of Final Warning

Confidential Memorandum

Date: [Current date]
To: [Employee]
From: [Manager] [Title]
Subject: Performance Problems—Final Warning

The intent of this memorandum is to follow up on our conversation of [date] regarding [problem], and to confirm that this discussion was a final warning.

As you know, we have had previous discussions regarding this issue. [Briefly summarize what was discussed, and when.] You also have received (a) written warning(s) about your unsatisfactory [performance/conduct].

Despite those efforts to move your [performance/conduct] back on track, you continue to [describe employee's continuing problems]. It is critical that [make expectations clear].

Please understand that this is a final warning. Any further unsatisfactory conduct or job performance on your part will result in your immediate dismissal.

I have read this final warning and have had the opportunity to discuss it with my manager. I understand that further unsatisfactory conduct or job performance on my part will result in my immediate termination.

Supervisor's Signature/Date

Employee's Signature/Date

Internal Investigation Outline

Internal Investigation Outline
Developed by Taren McCombs, HR Executive, SPHR

Section One: Background

(Briefly describe the facts giving rise to the investigation.)

For example: We understand from your supervisor that you have complained about certain behaviors that one of your colleagues have directed toward you. We also understand that you believe these behaviors may constitute sexual harassment. Because the organization views these matters very seriously, we are compelled to conduct an internal investigation—beginning with this interview.

Section Two: Investigation protocol

[Review the following with each person interviewed.]

Interviewer's role: We are conducting this interview to provide you with an opportunity to respond to information provided to Human Resources as a result of the complaint we received. The information that you provide us today may help us determine the appropriate course of action.

Confidentiality: We are committed to conducting a fair and objective investigation. Therefore, we will not draw any conclusions or make any recommendations until after we have obtained your responses.

We will only share the information that we obtain from you with those that have a legitimate business need to know.

[*For the complaining employee only:* You should be aware, however, that it may be necessary to discuss the information that you share with us with the accused and others, as appropriate and at the appropriate time.]

Retaliation: The organization will not tolerate retaliation or reprisals against anyone who shares knowledge or information during this investigation.

Factual Responses: You should be aware that anyone who intentionally provides false information or misdirects this investigation will be subject to disciplinary action, up to and including termination of employment. Accordingly, we will depend upon your open and honest responses to the questions that we ask today.

Section Three: Interview Questions

(Insert non-leading questions designed to clarify the issues in dispute. Provide interviewee with an opportunity to respond to all questions/allegations. Develop different questions for the complaining employee, alleged offender, and witnesses. *Do not* ask interviewees to draw conclusions. Seek facts only.)

Sample questions for a sexual harassment investigation:
- ✓ What happened?
- ✓ When did it happen?
- ✓ Who is the alleged harasser?
- ✓ When and where did the incident(s) take place?
- ✓ Were there any witnesses to the incidents?
- ✓ Were the incidents isolated or part of a continuing practice?
- ✓ What was the reaction of the complaining employee?
- ✓ How has the incident(s) affected the complaining employee personally and in the ability to perform work?
- ✓ Has the complaining employee discussed the matter with anyone else?
- ✓ Is there any documentation related to the incidents (for example, e-mails, letters, or voice mail)?

Closing Question: To help us ensure a fair and objective investigation into this matter is there anything else that you would like to tell us?

Section Four: Closing Comments

Review notes for accuracy and obtain the employee's signature and date below.

✓ Reinforce Confidentiality: Again, we will limit the disclosure of this information to those who have a legitimate business need to know. Likewise, we ask that you keep this information confidential and that you do not discuss this matter with anyone.

✓ Follow Up: We may need to follow up with you during the investigation and your continued cooperation may be necessary to help reach a resolution. Please feel free to contact me should you remember any additional information or if new information becomes available.

✓ Next Steps: We will continue to speak with others as necessary to reach a fair determination regarding next steps. Once we make a determination and share recommendations with (insert title of appropriate party), we will advise you of the outcome of the investigation.

I have had the opportunity to confirm my responses to the above questions and the contents accurately reflect my conversation with (insert interviewer's name).

Signature (Interviewee)/Date

Exit Interview Form

Companies often conduct interviews with exiting employees in order to understand the real reasons employees leave and to obtain information on processes, people, and departments that might need some redirection. If this valuable information is analyzed and necessary changes are made, employee turnover can be reduced.

Here are some sample questions you might consider:

- ✓ Why are you leaving?
- ✓ What did you like most about your job?
- ✓ If you could improve the job in any way, what would you suggest?
- ✓ How did you feel about the general working conditions at XYZ Organization?
- ✓ Did you think your pay was fair?
- ✓ What did you think of the benefits?
- ✓ Are there any benefits that you feel we should be offering that we currently are not?
- ✓ How would you describe the morale in your workgroup?
- ✓ How would you describe the morale at XYZ Organization in general?
- ✓ Using the scale of Excellent/Good/Fair/Poor, how would you rate the following items relative to your job?
  - → Cooperation within your workgroup.
  - → Cooperation from other workgroups.
  - → Communication within your workgroup.
  - → Communication with other workgroups.
  - → Opportunity for advancement.
- ✓ Using the scale of Excellent/Good/Fair/Poor, how would you rate the following items relative to your supervisor?
  - → Providing you with necessary information to perform your job efficiently and effectively.

→ Providing you with necessary training.

→ Providing you with recognition on the job.

→ Assisting with your career development.

→ Creating an environment of cooperation and team-work.

→ Providing you with frequent coaching and balanced feedback.

→ Encouraging and listening to your suggestions.

→ Resolving complaints and problems effectively.

→ Following policies and procedures.

✓ Would you recommend that a friend or acquaintance apply for a job here? Why or why not?

✓ If you could change three things about your department and three things about the organization, what would they be?

✓ Where are you going to work?

✓ What will your job responsibilities be?

✓ What appears better to you in your new position compared to your position with us?

✓ Additional comments:

Federal Labor Laws by Number of Employees

This chart identifies federal labor laws that apply to an employer based on its total number of employees. Several other factors may apply in determining employer coverage. Employers should review the laws to determine other criteria that may apply in determining employer coverage and should always consult with their labor attorney on employment law matters.

All employers

American Taxpayer Relief Act of 2012
Consumer Credit Protection Act of 1968
Employee Polygraph Protection Act (1988)
Employee Retirement Income Security Act (ERISA) (1974) (if organization offers benefits)
Equal Pay Act of 1963
Fair & Accurate Credit Transactions Act (FACT) of 2003
Fair Credit Reporting Act of 1969
Fair Labor Standards Act (FLSA) (1938)
Federal Income Tax Withholding
Federal Insurance Contributions Act of 1935 (FICA) (Social Security)
Health Insurance Portability and Accountability Act (HIPPA) of 1996 (if company offers benefits)
Immigration and Nationality Act (INA)
Immigration Reform & Control Act (IRCA) (1986)
Labor-Management Relations Act (Taft-Hartley) (1947)
Lilly Ledbetter Fair Pay Act of 2007
Management Relations Act
Mental Health and Addiction Equity Act of 2008 (for group health insurance plans)
National Labor Relations Act
National Labor Relations Act (NLRA) (1947)
Newborns' and Mothers' Health Protection Act of 1996
Occupational Safety & Health Act (OSHA) (1970)

OSHA Hazard Communication Standard
Sarbanes-Oxley Act of 2002
Uniform Guidelines of Employee Selection Procedures (1978)
Uniformed Services Employment and Reemployment Rights Act of 1994

More than fifteen employees

Civil Rights Act of 1964 Title VII, Civil Rights Act of 1991
Genetic Information Nondiscrimination Act (GINA) of 2008
Pregnancy Discrimination Act
Title I, Americans with Disabilities Act of 1990 (ADA)

More than twenty employees

Age Discrimination in Employment Act (1967) (ADEA)
Consolidated Omnibus Budget Reconciliation Act of 1986 (COBRA)

More than fifty employees

Affirmative Action Program (AAP)
Affordable Care Act (ACA)
Family and Medical Leave Act of 1993 (FMLA)
EEO-1 Report filed annually w/EEOC if organization is a federal contractor

More than one hundred employees

Worker Adjustment and Retraining Notification Act of 1989 (WARN)

Federal contractors

Contract Work Hours and Safety Standards Act (CWHSSA)
Copeland Act of 1934
Davis Bacon Act of 1931
Drug Free Workplace Act of 1988
Executive Orders 11246 (1965), 11375 (1967), 11478 (1969), 13201 (2001)
McNamara-O'Hara Service Contract Act (SCA)
Vietnam-Era Veterans Readjustment Act of 1974
Vocational Rehabilitation Act of 1973, Section 503

Walsh-Healy Act of 1936

War Hazards Compensation Act of 1942 (employees working overseas)

Federal and state posting requirements

Federal posting requirements

Many federal employment laws administered by the US Department of Labor (DOL) require notices to be posted in the workplace. The DOL publishes a Poster Advisor (*www.dol.gov*), which is designed to help employers comply with the poster requirements of several laws administered by the DOL. These laws require employers to display official DOL posters where employees can readily observe them. DOL provides the posters at no cost to the employers. The Poster Advisor only provides information about Federal DOL poster requirements. For information on your state's posting requirements, contact your state's Department of Labor.

OSHA poster

The *OSHA Job Safety and Health: It's the Law* poster is required to be displayed in every workplace in America. The poster informs employers and employees of their rights and responsibilities for a safe and healthful workplace and must be displayed in a conspicuous place where all employees can see it. If you are in a state with an OSHA-approved state plan, there may be a state version of the OSHA poster. Federal government agencies must use the Federal Agency Poster. See *www.OSHA.gov* for multiple ways to obtain the required posters.

Additional Resources

Associations

Association for Talent Development—leading association for workplace learning and performance professionals (*www.td.org*)

Human Resource Planning Society—global association of senior HR professionals in the world's leading organizations (*www.hrps.org*)

HRCI—premier credentialing organization for the HR profession (*www.hrci.org*)

Society for Human Resources Management—serves the needs of the human resource management professional by providing the most essential and comprehensive set of resources available (*www.shrm.org*)

WorldatWork—association dedicated to knowledge leadership in compensation, benefits, and total rewards (*www.worldatwork.org*)

Websites

www.hr.com

Largest community for HR professionals featuring articles, news, webcasts, forums, templates, and best practices of HR related subjects.

hrVillage

www.hrVillage.com

A destination for human resources professionals and those considering entering this career.

Department of Labor Wage and Hour Division

www.dol.gov

Fair Labor Standards Act

www.dol.gov

Management Library

A complete integrated online free management library for non-profits and for-profits.

www.managementhelp.org

Occupational Safety and Health Administration

www.osha.gov

Small Business Administration

www.sba.gov

GLOSSARY

Affirmative action: Any program, policy, or procedure an employer implements to correct past discrimination and prevent current and future discrimination in the workplace.

Affirmative action plan: A written affirmative action program that must be adopted pursuant to Executive Order 11246 by any non-construction contractor with fifty or more employees and federal government contracts of $50,000 or more.

Age Discrimination in Employment Act of 1967 (ADEA): A federal law applicable to employers of twenty or more employees, prohibiting discrimination based on age against employees or job applicants age forty or older (with no upper age limit) in favor of a younger person.

Americans with Disabilities Act of 1990 (ADA): A federal law applicable to employers of fifteen or more that bars discrimination against employees or job applicants because of their physical or mental disability; it requires the employer to provide reasonable accommodations to disabled individuals during both the hiring process and employment.

Baby Boomers: The generation born between 1946 and 1964.

Ban the box: A growing trend in employment law (already a requirement in some jurisdictions) to refrain from asking job candidates if they have a criminal record.

Behavioral interview: A carefully planned interview, based on the job and its outcomes, using the principle that past performance is the best indicator of future behavior. Specifically, it assumes that the way a job applicant has used his or her skills in the past will predict how he or she will use them in a new job. Interviewers should design questions to draw out candidates' stories of real-life experiences that illustrate their ability to perform the essential functions, reach the applicable goals, and excel in the job.

Benefits: Employer-provided "extras" other than pay that have financial value for employees.

Bereavement leave: Paid time off for an employee to attend the funeral of a family member or to attend to estate-related activities of a deceased family member.

BFOQ: Stands for "bona fide occupational qualification." It is a reason for taking an otherwise unlawful discriminatory action because the discrimination serves a legitimate business purpose. Examples include hiring only men to model male clothing and setting mandatory retirement ages for airline pilots.

Buddy system: The practice of matching new hires with more experienced employees to facilitate onboarding and training.

C-Suite: An organization's executive team, such as Chief Executive Officer (CEO), Chief Operating Officer (COO), Chief Financial Officer (CFO), and so on.

Cafeteria plan: A type of health care plan that allows employees to choose different types of health care benefits based on their individual needs.

Capital expenditure: Payment for the purchase, replacement, or expansion of facilities.

Career management system: A program intended to retain employees by helping them acquire and develop skills and abilities beyond those they already possess.

Career path: The progression of positions an employee moves through during his or her employment.

Chain of command: The order of positions according to responsibility and authority.

Coachable moment: Seizing the opportunity to speak up as soon as a manager sees behavior they like or dislike, as opposed to waiting for an annual review.

Compensation: Financial payment for work performed, as in wages and salaries.

Compensation philosophy: A statement about how an organization administers compensation. Ideally, it should explain the "why" behind all salary policies.

Competencies: Refers to a set of knowledge, skills, and abilities needed to perform a specific job.

Consolidated Omnibus Budget Reconciliation Act of 1986 (COBRA): A federal law granting certain former employees, retirees, spouses, ex-spouses, and dependent children the right to temporary continuation of health coverage at the pertinent organization's group rates.

Contingency planning: The process of identifying an organization's critical operating systems and how to keep them functioning in emergencies.

Corporate culture: The values, beliefs, and practices of an organization that directly influence the organization's, and its employees', conduct and behavior.

Corporate values: The most important principles of an organization; often joined with its mission statement.

Cost-per-hire: The direct and indirect costs incurred in filling a position.

Counseling: In a managerial context, supportive guidance to help an employee work through issues that affect job performance.

Crisis management: Organization-wide policies and procedures for responding to events such as natural disasters, product failures, or other events that threaten an organization or its operation.

Cultural orientation: The practice of using employee onboarding to acquaint new employees with organizational culture.

Data analytics: Applying analytic systems and processes to HR functions in order to improve performance, reduce turnover, increase productivity, and so on.

Data security: The protection of data from accidental or intentional unauthorized disclosure.

Development: Teaching employees the skills needed for current and future jobs.

Differentials: Unique compensation factors related to work time or locations, such as extra pay for working the graveyard shift or on an offshore oil rig.

Direct labor: People who actually produce or provide an organization's products or services.

Disciplinary action: Steps taken against an employee who fails to meet performance or behavioral standards.

Disengaged employee: One who is unhappy at work and who lets negativity show in words, attitudes, and actions.

Diversity: Differences like age, sexual orientation, race, religion, and similar categories among a group.

Dividend: Money or stock a company pays to its shareholders.

Downsizing: Reducing an organization's workforce by eliminating positions.

E-commerce: Paperless, electronic business transactions.

E-learning: Using webinars, videos, virtual reality, and other digital technologies for the purpose of training employees.

Employee Assistance Program (EAP): An employee benefit program (usually provided by an outside vendor) that helps employees with personal, psychological, or health problems that may affect their job performance.

Employee engagement: The managerial goal of fostering a workforce that is enthusiastic about, interested in, and fully committed to their jobs.

Employee Handbook or Manual: Written information covering the employer's policies and procedures.

Employee Referral Program: A program whereby employees are rewarded (financially or otherwise) for referring candidates for job openings.

Employee relations: A function of HR charged with discipline, termination, union regulations, and other aspects of maintaining fair treatment of employees.

Employee Retirement Income Security Act of 1974 (ERISA): A federal law setting minimum standards for pension plans in private industry.

Employee Self-service (ESS): In a highly-automated Human Resources department, employees can use ESS technology to get direct access to HR services.

Employee Stock Ownership Plan (ESOP): A trust established by the employer that operates as a tax-qualified, defined-contribution retirement plan, in which the employer's contributions are invested in company stock.

Employee Stock Purchase Plan: An employer-sponsored plan that lets employees buy company stock below its fair market price.

Employee training: Learning planned by the company to provide job-related knowledge, skills, abilities, and behaviors.

Employee turnover: The rate at which an organization loses employees due to resignation, retirement, or termination.

Employer of choice: An organization whose reputation and business practices make it such a great place to work that job applicants prefer it to another.

Employment-at-will: The employment law concept that both employers and employees can terminate the employment relationship at any time and for any lawful reason or for no reason.

Employment Cost Index (ECI): A statistic compiled by the federal government revealing changes in the cost of labor in the United States.

Engagement: How organizations create the conditions in which employees are committed to their jobs and employers.

Equal Employment Opportunity Commission (EEOC): The US agency that implements and enforces most federal antidiscrimination laws.

Equal Pay Act of 1963: A federal law requiring that men and women employed in the same establishment receive equal pay for work of equal effort, skill, and responsibility.

Ethics: The branch of knowledge that deals with moral principles, including correct conduct or behavior.

Exempt employees: Those employees who—because of their duties and mode or level of compensation—are exempt from the minimum wage and overtime pay requirements of the federal Fair Labor Standards Act (FLSA).

Exit interview: A meeting with a departing employee regarding his or her reason for leaving an organization and other observations on the person's experience there.

External audit: Assessment by an independent firm, based on generally accepted auditing procedures, to verify the accuracy of an organization's financial statements.

Fair Credit Reporting Act: A law (and supporting regulations) defining the ways consumer information derived from the files of consumer reporting agencies can fairly and lawfully be used.

Fair Labor Standards Act of 1938 (FLSA): A federal law establishing minimum wage, overtime pay, record-keeping, and child labor standards that affect full-time and part-time workers in the private sector, and in federal, state, and local governments.

Family and Medical Leave Act of 1993 (FMLA): A federal law providing the eligible employees of covered employers up to twelve weeks of unpaid leave in any twelve-month period for:

- ✓ The employee's own serious health condition.
- ✓ Taking care of a spouse, parent, or child with a serious health condition.
- ✓ The birth of a child to the employee.
- ✓ The employee's adoption or foster care of a child.

Federal Unemployment Tax Act (FUTA): An annual tax on the first $7,000 of wages paid to each employee.

Feedback: An ongoing workplace conversation about how well an employee is performing his or her job.

Fiduciary: A person, organization, or association that stands in a special relation of trust, confidence, or responsibility and is responsible for holding assets in trust for a beneficiary.

Flexible Spending Accounts (FSAs): A special account employees can put nontaxable money into for the purpose of paying certain out-of-pocket health care costs.

Form 5500 Annual Report: The annual return filed with the federal Employee Benefits Security Administration to report on employee pension and welfare benefit plans.

Form I-9: The government form that verifies an employee is legally qualified to work in the United States of America.

Gamification: The practice of using games to make employee orientation and training more engaging and enjoyable.

Gap analysis: Means of measuring and evaluating differences between a current position and what the organization wants it to become in the future.

General ledger: A financial book of final entry summarizing a company's financial transactions by offsetting debit and credit transactions.

Generation X: Employees born between 1965 and 1976.

Generation Z: Employees born after 1990.

Glass ceiling: A term for the barrier that prevents women and minorities from being widely represented in top positions at work.

Glassdoor.com: A job-search website where organizations can post job openings that is known for its extremely candid "reviews" of employers.

Globalization: The process of all countries becoming one community.

Governance: The ultimate action of management and leadership, often the function of a board of directors.

Health Insurance Portability & Accountability Act of 1996 (HIPAA): A federal law that safeguards health insurance continuity and the privacy of certain medical data for employees who change jobs and their dependents.

Health Maintenance Organization (HMO): A business that provides comprehensive health services for a flat fee.

HR analytics: The application of analytic processes within the HR profession.

HR metrics: Data used to quantify the cost and impact of talent management programs and HR processes.

Human Resource Information System (HRIS): The use of computer technology and customized software to fully automate HR functions, especially when it comes to minimizing paperwork, expediting services, and analyzing data.

Human resource management: Administering the policies, practices, and systems that affect employees in the workplace.

Inclusion: The state of being included or made a part of an organization or work group.

Independent Contractor: A nonemployee who provides services to an organization. It is vital for an employer to properly distinguish independent contractors from employees. If in any doubt, consult a labor lawyer.

Immigration Reform and Control Act of 1986 (IRCA): A federal law, applicable to employers of four or more employees, making it unlawful to hire any person not legally authorized to work in the United States; requiring employers to verify the employment eligibility of all new employees; and prohibiting discrimination on the basis of national origin or citizenship against any individual in the hiring or firing process.

Incentive pay: Variable compensation intended to motivate employees by paying for performance that exceeds expectations. Also known as "pay for performance."

Individual Personal Development Plan: A formal plan (nondisciplinary) for improving an employee's skills, performance, and career path.

Indeed: One of the most widely used online search engines in the US for job listings.

Job description: A written document detailing the requirements and responsibilities of a specific position.

Leveling: A technique used in determining compensation when the duties are significantly more or less responsible than those found in a salary survey.

LinkedIn: A social media platform for business purposes, especially useful for networking and recruiting.

Management: The responsibility for and control of an organization.

Manager Self-service (MSS): Managers can use MSS to get questions answered and problems solved with direct access to a highly-automated HR department. (See also Employee Self-service.)

Market lead, market lag, or meet-the-market strategy: The competitive position of your company when it comes to compensation.

Merit raise: A pay increase based on good performance.

Millennials: The generation of workers born between the years 1978 and 1990.

Mission statement: The written documentation of an organization's purpose.

National Labor Relations Act (NLRA): The foundational statute establishing the right of employees to form unions and engage in collective bargaining.

Negligent hiring: A legal claim available in some states, based on the theory that the employer should compensate a person who has been harmed by an individual the employer hired without exercising reasonable care.

Obamacare: See Patient Protection and Affordable Care Act.

Occupational Safety and Health Act of 1970: A federal law that imposes a general duty on employers to maintain a workplace free from recognized safety or health hazards, and establishes the Occupational Safety and Health Administration (OSHA).

Offshoring: The practice of relocating business processes to other countries where labor costs are lower than in the United States.

On-the-job training: Having a person learn job-related tasks by doing them.

Onboarding: The process of orienting new employees to the organization and to their new position.

Operating budget: A detailed list of all income and expenses during a specific period.

Organizational culture: The shared system of values, beliefs, assumptions, and traditions that govern the behavior of employees in an organization.

Orientation: A program designed by the company to inform new employees about its workplace, culture, policies, procedures, and benefits.

Occupational Safety and Health Administration (OSHA): An agency within the US Department of Labor that is responsible for establishing workplace safety standards and conducting inspections to ensure they are met.

Opioid crisis: Epidemic resulting from the rapid increase in the use of prescription and nonprescription opioid drugs.

Outsourcing: An employer's contracting with a third party that agrees to provide a service the employer previously provided for itself.

Overhead: Costs (excluding labor) associated with operating a business, including rent, utilities, taxes, and the like.

Paid Sick Leave Mandate: More and more states are requiring companies of a certain size to offer paid sick leave to part-time as well as full-time employees.

Paid time off: The tradition of paying employees during holidays, vacation, personal leave, and so on, in order to foster a mentally healthy workforce. (See also Paid Sick Leave Mandate.)

Patient Protection and Affordable Care Act: The proper name for "Obamacare," a significant overhaul, reform, and expansion of federal health care regulations and benefits.

Pay equity: The principle of paying employees equally for comparable work without regard to gender or other legally protected characteristics. Federal, state and local laws may well apply.

Pay grade: A designation or ranking of the pay for a group of similar jobs.

Pay range: Minimum to maximum pay for particular jobs as established by the employer. Ranges vary, depending on the job's level of authority and responsibilities and its market value.

Performance appraisal: Evaluation and discussion of an employee's job performance in relation to established objectives.

Performance management: The entire process of managing employee job performance, including setting goals, providing ongoing feedback, discussing job performance, and rewarding good work.

Personal Improvement Plan (PIP): A formal plan for improving the performance of an unsatisfactory employee in order to avoid discipline and/or termination.

Policy: Guidelines or rules on a specific issue, internal or external.

Pregnancy Discrimination Act of 1978: A federal law that amended Title VII of the Civil Rights Act of 1964 to clarify that discrimination on the basis of pregnancy, childbirth, or a related medical condition is a form of illegal sex discrimination. It requires that affected women be treated the same, for all employment-related purposes, as other employees or applicants with similar abilities or limitations.

Professional Employer Organization (PEO): An entity that enters into a joint-employment relationship with an employer by supplying it with employees.

Profit margin: Earnings expressed as a percentage of revenues.

Profit and loss statement: A financial document summarizing company revenue and expenses during a specific period of time.

Progressive discipline: A system of employee discipline that starts with less serious forms of discipline, such as oral counseling, for minor performance or conduct problems, and proceeds through more serious forms if needed, such as written warning, probation, or termination of employment.

Recruitment: Attracting appropriate candidates for an employer's job openings.

Reduction in force (RIF): An employee's or group of employees' involuntary separation from employment because of changing business needs such as economic pressures, lack of work, or organizational changes.

Reference check: Verification of an applicant's information about his or her work experience.

Retaliation: The unlawful act of disciplining, discriminating against, or terminating an employee who has taken legal action against an employer, expressed an intent to do so, or supported others pursuing their own legal claims.

Rightsizing: Prioritizing jobs or positions so as to identify and eliminate unnecessary ones.

Risk management: For HR and business purposes, the use of insurance or other investment strategies to minimize the employer's exposure to liability in the event of a loss or injury.

Salary compression: The unwanted effect on current employees when new employees (often with less experience) are hired at a higher salary.

Salary schedule: A way to reveal the pay range of all positions for companies that wish to be fully transparent with their employees about compensation.

Sarbanes Oxley Act of 2002 (SOX): A federal law enacted to increase the accountability of corporations to their shareholders in the wake of major accounting scandals. Many of its provisions are not germane to HR, but the act's whistleblower protection and 401(k) blackout-notice provisions are of note.

Sexual harassment: A form of gender discrimination that consists of unwelcome sexual advances; requests for sexual favors; or other verbal, visual, or physical conduct of a sexual or gender-biased nature that affects an individual's employment, unreasonably interferes with an individual's work performance, or creates an intimidating, hostile, or offensive work environment.

Statement of Work: A detailed, formal statement of needs and requirements on which prospective suppliers base their bids or proposals.

Strategic planning: Assembling a step-by-step "road map" needed to reach organizational goals.

Succession planning: Identifying long-range staffing needs and the internal or external candidates to fill them.

Telecommuting: A catchall term for using computer and telecommunications technology to work from a remote location, either full or part time.

Title VII of the Civil Rights Act of 1964 (Title VII): A federal law, applicable to employers of fifteen employees or more, prohibiting an employer from discriminating against employees or applicants based on race, color, gender, pregnancy, national origin, or religion.

Unemployment insurance: A government program that provides compensation to qualified workers during times of involuntary unemployment.

Veteran generation: Employees born before 1946.

Video interviews: A process whereby job candidates can record answers to interview questions on video for later review by HR and the hiring manager.

Virtual reality training: The use of virtual reality, augmented reality, and/or artificial intelligence systems for the purpose of training employees.

Virtual workforce: Employees who do not physically work in your place of business. They may work from home or from a location in a different part of the world.

W-2 form: The federal tax form employers give employees at the end of each calendar year, detailing total wages and withholdings.

W-4 form: The federal tax form that employees fill out and give to their employer so the organization can withhold the correct amounts of federal income tax from employees' pay.

Wage survey: A gathering of salary data from other companies to compare similar jobs in similar markets.

Wearable technology: The use of wearable devices (such as video cameras on police officers) for the purpose of training, management, and compliance.

Work/life balance: The balance an employee needs between time allocated for work and other aspects of their lives.

Workers' compensation: A state program that provides replacement income and medical expenses to employees who are injured or become ill because of their jobs, as well as financial benefits for the dependents and families of employees who die on the job.

Workforce planning: Assessment of an organization's current staffing and projections to meet future needs.

Zero-based budgeting: A method of budgeting in which every expenditure must be justified with each new budget, as opposed to the traditional method, in which only increases in expenditures over the previous budget must be justified.

FURTHER READING

Armstrong, Sharon. *The Essential Performance Review Handbook.* Pompton Plains, NJ: Career Press, 2010.

Armstrong, Sharon, and Madelyn Appelbaum. *Stress-free Performance Appraisals* (1st ed.). Franklin Lakes, NJ: Career Press, 2003.

Bliss, Wendy. *Legal, Effective References: How to Give and Get Them.* Richmond, VA: Society for Human Resource Management, 2001.

Branham, Leigh. *The 7 Hidden Reasons Employees Leave.* New York: AMACOM, 2005.

Buckingham, Marcus, and Curt Coffman. *First, Break All the Rules: What the World's Greatest Managers Do Differently.* New York: Simon and Schuster, 1999.

Buckingham, Marcus, and Donald Clifton. *Now, Discover Your Strengths.* New York: Simon and Schuster, 2001.

Burkholder, Nicholas, et al. *On Staffing—Advice and Perspectives from HR Leaders.* Hoboken, NJ: John Wiley & Sons, 2004.

Caruth, Donald L., and Gail D. Handlogten. *Managing Compensation (and Understanding It Too): A Handbook for the Perplexed.* Fairfield, CT: Quorum Books, 2001.

Chandler, Steve. *The Hands-Off Manager—How to Mentor People and Allow Them to Be Successful.* Franklin Lakes, NJ: Career Press, 2007.

Collins, Jim. *Good to Great.* New York: Harper Business, 2001.

Daniels, Aubrey. *Bringing Out the Best in People.* New York: McGraw-Hill, 1993.

Davis, Brian L., et al. *The Successful Manager's Handbook— Development Suggestions for Today's Managers.* Minneapolis, MN: Personnel Decisions International, 1992.

Drucker, Peter F. *The Practice of Management.* New York: Harper Business, 1986.

Eppler, Mark. *Management Mess-Ups—57 Pitfalls You Can Avoid (and Stories of Those Who Didn't).* Franklin Lakes, NJ: Career Press, 2005.

Fournies, Ferdinand F. *Coaching.* New York: McGraw-Hill, 2000.

Kohn, Stephen E., and Vincent D. O'Connell. *Six Habits of Highly Effective Bosses.* Franklin Lakes, NJ: Career Press, 2005.

Kouzes, James, and Barry Posner. *Leadership Challenge.* San Francisco, CA: Jossey-Bass, 2002.

Kushel, Gerald. *Reaching the Peak Performance Zone.* New York: AMACOM, 1994.

Levering, Robert. *A Great Place to Work.* New York: Harper Collins, 1990.

McKirchey, Karen. *Powerful Performance Appraisals.* Franklin Lakes, NJ: Career Press, 1998.

Mathis, Robert L., and John H. Jackson, *Human Resources Management* (12th ed.). Boston, MA: Cengage Publishing, 2008.

Miller, James, and Paul Brown. *The Corporate Coach: How to Build a Team of Loyal Customers and Happy Employees.* New York: Harper Business, 1994.

Mitchell, Barbara, and Cornelia Gamlem. *The Conflict Resolution Phrase Book.* Wayne, NJ: Career Press, 2017

Nail, Thomas, and Cornelia Gamlem. *Roadmap to Success: 5 Steps to Putting Action into Your Affirmative Action Program.* VA: Gem Publication, 2004.

Pfeffer, Jeffrey, and C. O'Reilly III. *Hidden Value: How Great Companies Achieve Extraordinary Results with Ordinary People.* Boston, MA: Harvard Business School Press, 2000.

Samit, Jay. *Disrupt You!* Stuttgart, Germany: Flatiron Books, 2015.

Sember, Brette McWhorter, and Terrence J. Sember. *The Essential Supervisor's Handbook.* Franklin Lakes, NJ: Career Press, 2007.

Sirota, David., et al. *The Enthusiastic Employee—How Companies Profit by Giving Workers What They Want.* Trenton, NJ: Wharton School Publishing, 2005.

Swan, William S. *How to Do a Superior Performance Appraisal.* New York: John Wiley & Sons, 1991.

Wilson, Jerry. *151 Quick Ideas to Inspire Your Staff.* Franklin Lakes, NJ: Career Press, 2007.

BIBLIOGRAPHY

Armstrong, Sharon. *The Essential Performance Review Handbook*. Pompton Plains, NJ: Career Press, 2010.

Armstrong, Sharon, and Madelyn Appelbaum. *Stress-free Performance Appraisals*. Franklin Lakes, NJ: Career Press, 2003.

———. "Baby Boomers Envision their Retirement," an AARP Segmentation Analysis conducted by Roper Starch Worldwide, Inc. and AARP, 1999.

Buckingham, Marcus, and Curt Coffman. *First, Break All the Rules—What the World's Greatest Managers Do Differently*. New York: Simon and Shuster, 1999.

Biro, Meghan M. *Five Ways Technology Is Changing the Face of HR*, Talent Culture Blog, February 4, 2016.

———. *HR Technology: A Revolution in the World of Work*. Forbes.com, April 23, 2013.

Caruth, Donald L., and Gail D. Handlogten. *Managing Compensation (and Understanding It Too)*. Fairfield, CT: Quorum Books, 2001.

DeNisi, Angelo S., and Ricky W. Griffin. *Human Resource Management.* Boston: Houghton Mifflin, 2001.

Dessler, Gary. *Human Resource Management.* Upper Saddle River, N.J: Prentice Hall, 2003.

Employee Self-Service Portals & Manager Self-Service Portals. Society of Human Resources Management (SHRM) white paper, *www.shrm.org*

Foulkes, Fred K. "The Expanding Role of the Personnel Function," quoted in John Ivancevich, *Human Resource Management.* New York: McGraw Hill, 2001.

Friedman, Dana. *Workplace Flexibility: A Guide for Companies.* Families and Work Institute website, 2002.

Haneberg, Lisa. *Facilitator's Guide: 10 Steps to Be a Successful Manager: Developing Managers for Success and Excellence.* Association for Talent Development, 2007.

Hankin, Harriet. *The New Workforce.* New York: AMACOM, 2005.

Hicks, Sabrina. "Successful Orientation Programs," in *Training and Development* (April 2000), quoted in Gary Dessler, *Human Resource Management.* Upper Saddle River, NJ: Prentice Hall, 2003.

"How Will New Technologies Change the Human Resources Profession." *www.indiana.edu/~jobtalk/HRMWebsite/hrm/articles/hrm/TechnologyChange.htm*

"How Will New Technologies Change the Human Resources Profession." *www.indiana.edu/~jobtalk/HRMWebsite/hrm/articles/hrm/TechnologyChange.htm*

IBM. "Sample Blogging & Social Media Policy." *www.ibm.com/blogs/zz/en/guidelines.html*

Ivancevich, John M. *Human Resource Management*, quoting Susan E. Jackson and Randall S. Schuler, "Understanding Human Resource Management in the Context of Organizations and Their Environments." New York: McGraw Hill, 2001.

Kovach, Kenneth A. *Strategic Human Resources Management.* Ocean City, MD: University Press of America, 1996.

Losey, Mike. *The Future of Human Resources.* Hoboken, NJ: John Wiley & Sons, 2005.

Lozar Glenn, Joanne. *Mentor Me: A Guide to Being Your Best Advocate in the Workplace.* Roanoke, VA: National Business Education Association, 2003.

Luhrs, Janet. "Making Work 'Work': New Ideas from the Winners of the Alfred P. Sloan Award for Business Excellence in Workplace Flexibility." Families and Work Institute, 2007.

———. *Market Pricing: Methods to the Madness.* Phoenix, AZ: WorldatWork, 2002.

———. *The Simple Life Guide.* New York: Broadway Books, 2001.

Martin, Carolyn A. *Managing Generation Y: Global Citizens Born in the Late Seventies and Early Eighties.* Cambridge, MA: HRD Press, 2001.

Mathis, Robert L., and John H. Jackson. *Human Resources Management* (12th ed.). New York: Cengage Publishing, 2008.

———. "Preparing for the Workplace of Tomorrow." San Francisco, CA: Hewitt Associates, 2004.

Mitchell, Barbara, and Cornelia Gamlem. *The Big Book of HR, Revised and Updated Edition* (Wayne, NJ: Career Press, 2017).

———. *The Essential Workplace Conflict Handbook.* Wayne, NJ: Career Press, 2015.

Redman, T., et al. "Performance Appraisal in an NHS Hospital," *Human Resource Management Journal,* 10 (2002): 48–62.

———. *Salary Budget Survey.* Phoenix, AZ: WorldatWork, annual.

Samit, Jay. "4 Ways Augmented Reality Could Change Corporate Training Forever." *Fortune.com,* July 22, 2017.

———. *Disrupt You!* New York: Flatiron Books, 2015.

Senge, Peter M. *The Fifth Discipline.* New York: Currency Doubleday, 1994.

Sirota, David, et al. *The Enthusiastic Employee—How Companies Profit by Giving Workers What They Want.* Upper Saddle River, NJ: Pearson Education, 2005.

———. "New Book from Wharton Publishing Exposes as Myths 33 Beliefs About Work and Workers." Sirota Myths and Findings Report 2005: Sirota Survey Intelligence.

———. *Survey Handbook & Directory: A Guide to Finding and Using Salary Surveys.* Phoenix, AZ: WorldatWork, 2006.

———. *2004 HR Outsourcing Survey Report.* Richmond, VA: SHRM, 2005.

"6 Technological Trends That Redefine Human Resource Management Financesonline.com," *https://financesonline.com/6-technological-trends-redefine-human-resource-management/*

Society of Human Resource Management. "Sample Social Media Policy." *www.shrm.org*

Winfrey, E. C., *Kirkpatrick's Four Levels of Evaluation* (1999), in B. Hoffman (Ed.), *Encyclopedia of Educational Technology.* Reprinted with permission. Retrieved July 3, 2007 at *http://coe.sdsu.edu*

NOTES

Introduction

1. Gary Dessler, *Human Resource Management.* Upper Saddle River, NJ: Prentice Hall, 2003, p. 2.

2. Interview. WRC-Radio, Washington, DC (Nov. 21, 2005).

Chapter 1

1. Barbara Mitchell and Cornelia Gamlem, *The Big Book of HR, Revised and Updated Edition* (Wayne, NJ: Career Press, 2017), p. 29.

Chapter 2

1. "The Perfect Want Ad: Funnel Candidates Who Fit the Job and the Culture," M-Live Media Group Blog.

2. Michael D. Haberman, "How to Improve the New Employee Experience," Webinar, *www.trainhr.com/ control/w_product/~product_id=702182LIVE/~Michael%20*

D._Haberman/~2-Hour_Virtual_Seminar_on_Onboarding_is_NOT_Orientation_-_How_to_Improve_the_New_Employee_Experience

3. "Use LinkedIn for Recruiting Employees," *The Balance.com, www.thebalance.com/use-linkedin-for-recruiting employees-1918950*

4. "5 Things You Can Do with a Glassdoor Free Employer Account," *Glassdoor.com, www.glassdoor.com/employers/blog/5-things-can-free-employer-account/*

5. "Tips for Employers on Glassdoor, Indeed, Vault, Etc.," Avid Technical Resources Blog, *www.avidtr.com*

6. "Indeed vs. Glassdoor: A Battle of Quality vs. Quantity," Digital Astronauts blog, *www.digital-astronauts.com/indeed-vs-glassdoor-battle-quality-vs-quantity/*

7. "The Rise of the Webcam Job Interview," *Chicago Tribune, www.chicagotribune.com/business/ct-careers-webcam-job-interview-20161017-story.html*

8. Allison Tinkham. "Video Job Interviews: Hiring Helper or Hindrance?" *Insperity.com* blog, *www.insperity.com/blog/video-job-interviews-hiring-helper-or-hindrance/*

9. "The Rise of the Webcam Job Interview," *Chicago Tribune, www.chicagotribune.com/business/ct-careers-webcam-job-interview-20161017-story.html*

10. Rebecca Knight, "The Right Way to Check Someone's References," *Harvard Business Review, https://hbr.org/2016/07/the-right-way-to-check-someones-references*

Chapter 3

1. Frank Birkel, et. al, "Executive Onboarding: Is There a Right Way?" SpencerStuart blog, *www.spencerstuart.com/research-and-insight/executive-onboarding*

2. Judith Brown, "Employee Orientation: Keeping New Employees On Board!" IPMA-HR white paper,

www.thebalancecareers.com/employee-orientation-keeping
-new-employees-on-board-1919035

3. Ibid.

4. Sabrina Hicks, "Successful Orientation Programs," in
   Training and Development (April 2000), quoted in Gary
   Dessler, *Human Resource Management* (Upper Saddle River,
   NJ: Prentice Hall, 2003).

5. Carter McNamara, "Orienting New Employees (New
   Hires, On-Boarding)," Free Management Library, *https://
   managementhelp.org/training/employee-orientation.
   htm#checklist*

6. "Stuck in a Recruitment Cycle? Rethink Your Induction
   Process," infographic, Quotient blog, *www.qotient.com/
   qblog/2016/2/19/stuck-in-a-recruitment-cycle-rethink-your
   -induction-process*

7. Jeff Haden. "4 Ways to Get a New Employee Off to a Perfect
   Start," *Inc.com, www.inc.com/jeff-haden/4-ways-to-get-a-new
   -employee-off-to-the-perfect-start.html*

8. "How to Write a Great Employee Handbook," National
   Federation of Independent Businesses (NFIB) blog, *www.
   nfib.com/content/resources/labor/how-to-write-a-great
   -employee-handbook/*

9. Ibid.

10. Frank Birkel, et. al., "Executive Onboarding: Is There a Right
    Way?" SpencerStuart blog, *www.spencerstuart.com/research
    -and-insight/executive-onboarding*

11. Sabrina Son, "10 Vital Steps for Onboarding an Executive,"
    TINYpulse blog, *www.tinypulse.com/blog/employee
    -onboarding-executive*

Chapter 4

1. Association for Talent Development, "State of the Industry
   Report," *www.td.org/Publications/Blogs/ATD-Blog/2016/12/
   ATD-Releases-2016-State-of-the-Industry-Report*

2. *www.ziglar.com/quotes/employees/*

3. Lisa Haneberg, *Facilitator's Guide: 10 Steps to Be a Successful Manager: Developing Managers for Success and Excellence* (Association for Talent Development, 2007).

4. Sarah Johnson, "Finding Common Ground: How to Effectively Train Different Generations," Knowledge Anywhere Blog, *www.knowledgeanywhere.com/resources/ article-detail/how-to-effectively-train-different-generations*

5. Barbara Mitchell and Cornelia Gamlem, *The Big Book of HR, Revised and Updated Edition* (Wayne, NJ: Career Press, 2017).

6. Joanne Lozar Glenn, *Mentor Me: A Guide to Being Your Best Advocate in the Workplace* (Roanoke, VA: National Business Education Association, 2003).

7. James Madison University Human Resources Department, "Performance Management," *www.jmu.edu/humanresources/ hrc/performance/ipdp.shtml*

8. United States Department of Labor, OSHA website, "Workplace Violence," *www.osha.gov/SLTC/ workplaceviolence/*

9. Ibid.

10. "How to Manage Bullying in the Workplace," Workplace Answers blog, *www.workplaceanswers.com/resources/hr -article-library/how-to-manage-bullying-in-the-workplace/*

11. E. C. Winfrey, *Kirkpatrick's Four Levels of Evaluation* (1999), in B. Hoffman (Ed.), *Encyclopedia of Educational Technology.* Reprinted with permission. Retrieved July 3, 2007.

12. Peter Senge, *The Fifth Discipline: The Art & Practice of The Learning Organization* (New York: Currency Doubleday, 1994).

Chapter 5

1. Derek Thompson, "The Case Against Performance Reviews," *The Atlantic*, January 29, 2014, *www.theatlantic.com/business/archive/2014/01/the-case-against-performance-reviews/283402/*

2. Vauhini Vara, "The Push Against Performance Reviews," *The New Yorker*, July 24, 2015, *www.newyorker.com/business/currency/the-push-against-performance-reviews*

3. Dana Wilkie, "Is the Annual Performance Review Dead," Society for Human Resource Management, *www.shrm.org*

4. Vauhini Vara, "The Push Against Performance Reviews," *The New Yorker*, July 24, 2015, *www.newyorker.com/business/currency/the-push-against-performance-reviews*

5. Dana Wilkie, "Is the Annual Performance Review Dead," Society for Human Resource Management, *www.shrm.org*

6. Jane McGregor, "Study Finds that Basically Every Single Person Hates Performance Reviews," *Washington Post*, January 27, 2014, *www.washingtonpost.com/news/on-leadership/wp/2014/01/27/study-finds-that-basically-every-single-person-hates-performance-reviews/?utm_term=.84c69f44bb0a*

7. Mike Losey, "Creating a Culture of Constant Feedback," Smart HR, Inc. blog, June 28, 2017 *www.smarthrinc.com/2017/06/creating-feedback-culture/*

8. Dana Wilkie, "Is the Annual Performance Review Dead," Society for Human Resource Management, *www.shrm.org*

9. Vauhini Vara, "The Push Against Performance Reviews," *The New Yorker,* July 24, 2015, *www.newyorker.com/business/currency/the-push-against-performance-reviews*

10. Ibid.

Chapter 6

1. *www.ahip.org*

2. *www.shrm.org*

3. *https://eligibility.com/state-disability-insurance*

4. US Bureau of Labor Statistics, "Employer Costs for Compensation," news release, June 21, 2006, found at *www.bls.gov*

Chapter 7

1. "Survey Handbook & Directory: A Guide to Finding and Using Salary Surveys," (WorldatWork 2006).

2. "Market Pricing: Methods to the Madness," at 80 (WorldatWork, 2002).

Chapter 8

1. Sharon Armstrong and Madelyn Applebaum, *Stress-free Performance Appraisals* (Franklin Lakes, NJ: Career Press, 2003).

Chapter 10

1. Barbara Mitchell and Cornelia Gamlem, *The Essential Workplace Conflict Handbook* (Wayne, NJ: Career Press, 2015), p. 40–41.

2. Laura Sherbin and Ripa Rasid, "Diversity Doesn't Stick Without Inclusion," *Harvard Business Review,* February 1, 2017.

Chapter 11

1. Meghan M. Biro, "HR Technology: A Revolution for the World of Work," *Forbes.com*, April 23, 2013, *www.forbes.com/sites/meghanbiro/2013/04/28/hr-technology-a-revolution-for-the-world-of-work/#79e46a5c178b*

2. "Managing Flexible Work Arrangements," Society for Human Resource Management, *www.shrm.org*

3. "Employee Self-Service Portals & Manager Self-Service Portals," Society for Human Resource Management (SHRM) white paper, *www.shrm.org*

4. Meghan M. Biro, "5 Ways Technology Is Changing the Face of HR," Talent Culture blog, February 4, 2016.

5. Ibid.

6. Jay Samit, "4 Ways Augmented Reality Could Change Corporate Training Forever," *Fortune.com*, July 22, 2017, *http://fortune.com/2017/07/22/augmented-reality-corporate-training/*

7. "6 Technological Trends that Redefine Human Resource Management," Financesonline.com, *https://financesonline.com/6-technological-trends-redefine-human-resource-management/*

8. Ibid.

9. "How Will New Technologies Change the Human Resources Profession," *www.indiana.edu/~jobtalk/HRMWebsite/hrm/articles/hrm/TechnologyChange.htm*

10. IBM, "Sample Blogging & Social Media Policy," *www.ibm.com/blogs/zz/en/guidelines.html*

11. Society for Human Resource Management, "Sample Social Media Policy," *www.shrm.org*

Chapter 12

1.   Barbara Mitchell and Cornelia Gamlem, *The Big Book of HR, Revised and Updated Edition* (Wayne, NJ: Career Press, 2017), p. 113.

2.   Sharon Armstrong and Madelyn Appelbaum, "Baby Boomers Envision Their Retirement," an AARP Segmentation Analysis conducted by Roper Starch Worldwide, Inc. and AARP, 1999, p. 6.

3.   Harriet Hankin, *The New Workforce* (New York: AMACOM, 2005).

4.   David Sirota, et al. *The Enthusiastic Employee—How Companies Profit by Giving Workers What They Want* (Upper Saddle River, NJ: Pearson Education, 2005).

5.   Meghan M. Brio, "Data Security Must Be a Top Priority for HR," *Huffington Post*, Dec. 6, 2017.

INDEX

ABOUT THE AUTHORS

Sharon Armstrong began her career in human resources in 1985 as a recruiter and trainer at a large Manhattan law firm, where she was promoted to a managerial role within six months. Following that position, she was director of Human Resources at another law firm and at three nonprofit associations in Washington, DC.

Since launching Sharon Armstrong and Associates in 1998, she has consulted with many large corporations and small businesses. She has provided training and completed HR projects for a wide variety of clients in the profit and nonprofit sectors as well as in government. She now runs a talent brokering agency for HR, OD, Trainers, Coaches, and Keynote speakers (*www.trainersandconsultants.net*).

Sharon received her BA *cum laude* from the University of Southern Maine and her master's degree in counseling from George Washington University. A certified Professional in Human Resources, she is a member of the national Society for Human Resource Management and its local chapter.

Barbara Mitchell is an author, speaker, and is the managing partner of The Mitchell Group, a human resources and organizational development consulting practice. She consults with a wide variety of clients on issues involving people, helping them successfully hire, develop, engage, and retain the best talent available. Most of her HR career was spent in senior leadership positions with Marriott International, Human Genome Sciences, and as co-owner and Principal of The Millennium Group, LLC.

She is a graduate of North Park University, Chicago, Illinois, with a degree in history and political science. She has taken graduate-level business courses at UCLA, the University of Denver, and Loyola University.

Barbara is a video presenter/docent at the Smithsonian's American Art Museum and is a past member of the executive committee of the board of directors of the Northern Virginia Habitat for Humanity affiliate. She resides in the Washington, DC, metro area.

Stay Connected with Sharon and Barbara

Visit our websites
www.bigbookofhr.com
www.essentialworkplaceconflicthandbook.com
www.trainersandconsultants.net

Read our weekly blog
makingpeoplematter.blogspot.com

Follow us on Twitter
@bigbookofhr
@gotworkconflict
@saanetwork

Other books by these authors
Sharon Armstrong
The Essential Performance Review Handbook
Stress-free Performance Appraisals
Heeling the Canine Within: The Dog's Self-Help Companion

Barbara Mitchell and Cornelia Gamlem
The Big Book of HR
The Essential Workplace Conflict Handbook
The Conflict Resolution Phrase Book
The Manager's Answer Book

All of our books are available on Amazon.com. If you've enjoyed what you've read, we would be grateful for a positive review. Thank you!